Copyright © 2018
Mary E. Heath

All rights reserved. This is a work of fiction. Any resemblance to persons living or dead is purely coincidental. No part of this book may be used or reproduced in any manner whatsoever without written permission from the author, except in the case of brief quotations embodied in critical articles and for review purposes. References to real people, events, establishments, organizations, or locations are intended only to provide a sense of authenticity.

Syzgos—

Hope you enjoy it!

Love,
Mary
May

Faith's Legacy

Saving Gideon

(The Angel Chronicles)

Faith's Legacy

By Mary May

Table of Contents

Angel Cast List
Chapter 1
Chapter 2
Chapter 3
Chapter 4
Chapter 5
Chapter 6
Chapter 7
Chapter 8
Chapter 9
Chapter 10
Chapter 11
Chapter 12
Chapter 13
Chapter 14
Chapter 15
Chapter 16
Chapter 17
Chapter 18
Chapter 19
Chapter 20
Chapter 21
Chapter 22
Chapter 23
Chasing Hope

Angel Cast List

Gideon- Charlie
Shana- Nate
Charlotte- Sabrina
Zareck- Devon
Raphael- Luke
Skye- D.J.
Kavik- Cleo
Baylor- Catherine
Anthony- Evan
Donavan- Carl
Evie- Keelie
Leia- Kinsley
Mac- SA (Special Assignment) angel

Chapter 1

Nate pulled Charlie down one hall then another of the massive hospital. The halls all looked the same to her now, although not too long ago she knew them like the back of her hand. He finally stopped at a nurse's desk that she actually recognized.

"Hey, this was your hall and your room was right over there!" She smiled as she pointed it out to him. Try as she might, she couldn't quite shake some of the terrible memories that came flooding back.

"Charlie? I'm sorry…I promise I won't ever hurt you like that again." Nate's face clearly showed his regret for causing her pain. Even if he did feel he was doing it for the right reasons.

"I know that, Nate…I really do."

He kissed her forehead then smiled as he saw Dr. Reed coming down the hall.

"Nate! Charlie! It's wonderful to see you both!" He shook Nate's hand then hugged Charlie warmly. He smiled down at the golden wedding bands on their hands.

"I see that you accomplished what you set out to do, to win the hand of this lovely lady."

Nate grinned. "I did. It took some doing and some divine intervention, but I lucked out."

Charlie poked him in the chest. "You were blessed out, you mean!"

"So how are things around here? Is Hattie around? I would love for her to meet Charlie."

"Well, I think she may be here somewhere. I haven't had to assign her to anyone since you left. Everyone else had the good sense to listen." He picked up a phone and paged the nurse.

Charlie gave Nate a snarky grin.

"Hey, at least you're known for something, right?"

"Oh, you're funny…seriously."

Mac laughed as he stood next to Gideon and Shana. "I think she is."

Shana nodded in agreement. "That's why Charlie is so good for Nate -- she keeps him humble." They all turned when they heard the quick steps of Hattie coming down the hallway.

"Nathaniel! It's wonderful to see you!" Her face was all smiles as she wrapped Nate in a big hug. Turning to Charlie, she asked, "Now just who is this pretty thing? This isn't the Charlie that I heard so much about, is it?"

Nate smiled with pride as he wrapped his arm around her shoulders. "Hattie, I would like for you to meet Charlie Jackson."

The woman's brows rose into her hairline. "Jackson, is it?"

Nate grinned. "Yup...she is my wife as of three days ago."

Hattie once more looked shocked. "Three days? For the love of Moses! This is where you brought the young lady for her honeymoon? Nathaniel Jackson! That's shameful!" she scolded.

He held up his hand as if to fend her off when she threatened to smack him.

"Hold on! I brought her to *California* for the honeymoon. I brought her *here* for a visit."

Hattie's face brightened. "Oh! Well, that's different. Congratulations!"

Charlie smiled. "Thank you. I have heard so much about Nurse Hattie that I was dying to meet you. I know you are the reason that Nate gave his heart to Christ. Thank you so much." She reached out, placing her hand on the nurse's arm.

"Oh, no thanks is necessary, my dear. The Lord would have found someone to get through that thick blockhead of his...Lucky me, I just happened to be handy."

Mac roared with laughter. "Ok, now, this lady is hilarious!"

Nate shot him a dark look.

"Hey, that's funny. I don't care who you are!" the angel said with another snort of laughter.

"Why don't we all go to my office where we can visit?" Dr. Reed suggested.

They were walking down the hall when the doctor's name was called over the hospital intercom. Throwing them an apologetic glance, he told Hattie to take care of them while he tended to the emergency; then he took off down the hall.

"I hope everything will be alright," Charlie said to Nate as they walked into Dr. Reed's office. "What did that mean, Hattie?"

Sitting on the corner of the doctor's desk, she gave them a grave look. "It means a patient has coded. It's been happening frequently…too frequently, if you ask me."

Nate frowned. "Like how frequently?"

"Almost daily…sometimes more than once a day. It's very unsettling. We have patients code from time to time. This is a hospital with severely-wounded and ill people, so it's to be expected to some extent. But lately it's been really excessive."

Gideon looked at Shana who looked at Mac who looked at Nate.

"Are all the codes resulting in deaths?" Charlie asked.

Hattie shook her head.

"No, but a lot of them are. We have an inspector and a committee coming down to look things over. It really doesn't bode well for this hospital." When another alert rang out over the intercom, Hattie got quickly to her feet.

"I'm sorry, but I need to go."

"Don't worry about us. We know our way out and we will catch up with you later," Nate assured her; then he turned to Charlie when he spoke. "That really doesn't sound good, does it? What do you think could be causing all the patients to code like that?"

"I don't know but I hope they figure it out."

He nodded his head to Mac who then left to go find out what was going on in the hospital.

Later that night, Mac returned. Shana and Gideon were the only ones still awake. "So, did you find out anything?"

The SA angel nodded, his usual megawatt smile absent. "Yeah, we have a serious problem. The patients are not coding from natural causes."

"I didn't figure they were. My wings were bristling from the moment we stepped into the hospital. It had a different feel to it this time. Were you able to spot the culprit?"

Nodding slowly, Mac looked at Gideon.

"I'm afraid so… you won't believe who it is."

Shana looked from one male to the other.

"Who is it?"

"It's Gideon's old friend Karau."

Gideon looked at him blankly. "I don't know who that is."

Mac nodded, and then he leaned against the wall.

"You probably know him better by what he does than by what he is actually called. Let me put it to you this way. Does the thought of a vat of boiling iron make you break out in a cold sweat?"

Gideon's eyes clashed with Mac's. While the thought of a boiling vat didn't make him break out into a cold sweat, it did make his wrists ache with the ghastly memory of swinging over one…

Faith's Legacy

Minutes later Gideon finished telling the other angels about his encounter with Karau. Shana's eyes grew wide as she glanced down at Gideon's thick wrists.

"Wow! I can't believe that Zareck was able to get to you in time! He must have flown faster than any angel has ever flown before!"

Gideon nodded. "Yeah, pretty much, and that answered my question of why he was around for all of this. The Creator knew that no other angel would have been able to do it."

Mac nodded as his face kept its unusual serious expression. "If that is what this thing is capable of, we have to destroy it."

"But how? We don't even know what it's doing here; not only that, we don't know how long we are going to be here. What if we are not here long enough to help?" Shana pointed out.

Mac shook his head. "I will talk to Nate and explain that this may need to be an extended visit."

Gideon didn't say anything, but staying was the last thing he wanted to do. The further away he could keep Charlie from Karau, the better he would feel...

The next morning Charlie woke up, stretching her arms high above her head, when her yawn suddenly turned into a gasp when Nate's sneaky hands found her ribs.

"Stop it!" she said as she swatted at him.

Grinning from his side of the bed, Nate shook his head as he focused on his attack.

"I'm warning you, Nate Jackson! You better get ready to get as good as you give!" Charlie warned as she got to her knees to better protect her ticklish ribs.

"No, ma'am, I was taught to never surrender," Nate replied. A devilish glint sparkled in his dark brown eyes.

Without warning he pounced, knocking Charlie flat on her back as his hands tickled her ribs ruthlessly. Charlie laughed and squealed as she tried to squirm her way out from under Nate's body. Finally, she was able to slip her hand past his and went in for the kill shot, finding Nate's one weak spot just above his hipbone. Falling backwards from her sneak attack, Nate cried out for mercy as Charlie straddled his hips, tickling until he was totally incapacitated. Reaching up, he captured her wrists then easily flipped her over until she stared up at him. Dropping a quick kiss on her nose, he smiled.

"I love you, Mrs. Nate Jackson," he whispered.

"Yeah…yeah… but do you surrender?" Charlie asked with an arched brow.

Nate chuckled as he looked down at Charlie, who was clearly in no position to be declared the victor, and shook his head. "I surrendered to you a long time ago, lady. I don't even know what I was thinking," he replied with a self-mocking look.

Charlie gave him a bright smile that made his insides do flip-flops. "I love you, too, Mr. Jackson." Once Nate had let her up, she asked, "What are our plans for today?"

Nate rolled off and settled Charlie into the crook of his arm. "I was thinking of going back to the hospital. We really didn't get a chance to visit with anyone yesterday with all the code alarms going off."

Charlie propped her head up on her hand so she could see Nate's face. "What was up with that? Did you get the same weird vibe I got when they were telling us about it?"

Nate nodded. "Yeah, I did. That's another reason why I want to go back. I don't know what we can do, but I have this feeling that we should be there."

After breakfast, they returned to the hospital to find the floor that Nate used to be on in complete chaos. Nurses were running down the hall and into various rooms. Medical codes were being blasted from the intercom one after another. Nate and Charlie stood watching all the commotion in shock. Charlie spotted Dr. Reed coming out of a room three doors down from where they were standing. He looked exhausted with dark circles under his eyes and a face lined with worry. He gave them a brief smile when he saw them.

Faith's Legacy

"I'm sorry, Nate -- Now isn't a good time for a visit. As you can see, things are pretty hectic around here."

"Has it been like this all morning?" Charlie asked.

"Since last night before midnight. We have lost three patients and I'm afraid there will be more. I'm sorry I can't talk. I have to go." With an apologetic glance, he hurried down the hall to where a nurse was waving at him from the doorway of yet another patient's room.

Charlie turned to Nate. "My gosh, what on earth do you think is going on?"

"I don't know but it sure seems odd," Nate answered as he looked past Charlie to where Mac was standing. Seeing the nod that Mac gave him toward the men's room, he excused himself and followed the angel inside. Nate was relieved to see it was a single-user restroom. The last thing he needed was for someone to hear him talking to someone they couldn't see.

"Did you find out anything last night?" Nate asked without wasting time.

"I did, and Nate... it's not good." Mac told him everything he had found out, finishing with a sigh.

Nate's face well told how he felt. "So, what can we do to help?"

"I'm not sure, but we need to stay here for a while. Can you arrange that without telling Charlie why?"

Nate slowly nodded his head. "She already knows something is going on, so that won't be a problem. What can Charlie and I do to help?"

"Right now, pray! Pray for protection for the patients and the hospital staff. I will let you know if there is anything more you can do."

After Mac disappeared, Nate left the restroom and went down the hall to the waiting room. It was empty except for Charlie, and she already had her head bowed in prayer. She looked up when she heard Nate sit down next to her.

"I just felt this overwhelming need to pray for the hospital and all the patients." She placed her hand over her heart. "I haven't felt such an intense need to pray since the day I found out about your accident."

Faith's Legacy

Nate reached out and took her hand in his. "I feel the same way. There is something very evil having its way in this hospital. Do you feel it?"

"Yes, I do! I have felt it from the moment we walked in yesterday. It didn't feel like this before when you were in here. What can we do?"

"For now, we pray and we watch. When we get a chance, I want to talk with Dr. Reed and Hattie. Find out what they think is going on."

"I think we should call Mama and Devon, too. Let's get them to praying and tell them to start a prayer chain," Charlie suggested. "But let's pray together right now."

Nate held Charlie's hand as they both bowed their heads and went before the Lord in prayer.

Chapter 2

Deep below the hospital, down in the recesses of the earth, a group of demons were all crowded together in a small natural cavern. The demon leader, Karau, was giving out orders to the lesser-ranked minions when he suddenly lifted his head and spread wide his nostrils. As he inhaled deeply, the deep red of his eyes glowed in anger.

"What is that?" he asked as he continued to smell the air.

The other demons in the cave all started sniffing the air, trying to determine the scent and where it was coming from.

All at once Karau bellowed as he reached out and raked black talons across the granite walls, leaving deep gouges in his wake. "Someone is praying...and they are praying with *faith*! Who is it?" Spittle flew from his mouth as if the very words were an abomination to his existence.

A smaller demon bowed before him, the tips of his thin leathery wings scraping the ground in abject humility. Not daring to lift his eyes, he spoke.

"My lord, I did receive word that a few new angels appeared on the hospital grounds yesterday afternoon. I didn't want to bother you because they had been here before and caused us little trouble."

Karau slowly turned his head to look at the little demon that was still staring at the ground in a posture of humility.

"What kind of angels were they?" he asked.

"Two guardians and a Special Assignment, sir," the demon quickly replied.

In the corner, another demon approached Karau, his head lifted slightly higher than the smaller one.

"Sir, if I may?" He waited for his leader's approval before coming any closer.

Karau inclined his head slightly, giving him permission to approach.

"Sir, what the other told is a lie. There were three angels, one Special Assignment and one guardian."

Karau stared at the other demon calmly with an arched brow. "That's only two, do we know what the third angel was?"

The demon nodded his head. "Yes, sir. It was a warrior angel."

Karau cocked his head to one side. "Interesting, but not particularly alarming."

The demon raised his hand once more, looking for permission to speak.

"What?" Karau demanded with barely-veiled hostility.

"Sir, there is just one more thing I feel you should know. "

"What is it?" Karau snapped.

"Sir, the warrior angel is...well, I'm nearly positive that it was..." The demon stammered until Karau couldn't take it.

"**Who was it?**" he roared, making the rest of the demons cower and back up as far as the cave walls would let them.

"Gideon, sir. It was Gideon the Mighty."

There was a collective hiss that went through the cave at the mention of the warrior's name, but Karau only smiled, if the slight stretching of his thin lips could be called that.

"Gideon the Mighty, you say? Well...well...well... so we meet again."

Gideon walked along behind Shana. They followed Nate and Charlie from the hospital. He kept his eyes moving in a constant circle pattern. He would sweep the ceiling then down the hall in front of them and then he would check behind him. The tingle in his wings and running down his spine alerted him to the fact that the hospital was overrun with demons. Every building where humans gather generally has a few evil minions, but this time they were gathered up in a very large number; it wasn't just the number that had him concerned -- it was the ranks. There were high-ranking demons gathered nearby. Mac dropped back to walk next to Gideon.

"Man! It's bad, really bad! I'm not even a warrior and my wings are tingling like crazy with the need to sharpen. It was nothing like this when we were here before."

Gideon nodded as he kept quartering and searching the area as they left the hospital. "I agree it wasn't like this when I was here last either. But that doesn't matter. They are here now."

"I've done a little research on Karau," Mac added. "It seems that he is the leader over rebellion. Wherever you find uprisings and people trying to overthrow governments and leaders, you will find Karau."

"So, why is he at a hospital? If this was a house of legislation, I could understand it." This came from Shana who had also dropped back to join their conversation.

"This isn't just a hospital; it's a military hospital. Perhaps he is trying to cause an uprising in the military somehow," Mac offered. "What do you think, Gideon?"

Gideon was silent as he thought about everything that Mac had just told him. "I think he is doing this in phases. He is after something big, and this is his first step. If he takes out the military, then what's stopping him from taking out anything else? We need to keep watchful eyes on the world news. That might give us a clue what he is up to."

Charlie nodded as she listened to her mother on the other end of the phone. They had just returned to their hotel room and she immediately called her parents to tell them of the strange deaths at the hospital. She hung up a few minutes later after Sabrina had promised to start a prayer chain. She also said a hasty prayer of protection over Nate and Charlie.

Charlie walked over to Nate, who was standing staring out of the window, but she knew his mind wasn't on the beautiful view that lay beyond the glass.

"I don't know what to do, Charlie. If I was still in the East, I would know how to fight the enemy, but here those skills are useless to me."

Charlie wrapped her arms tightly around Nate's waist, leaning her head against his broad back. "The Bible says that we fight not against flesh and blood, but against powers and principalities in the air. So, our weapons are not carnal weapons. We fight with our spiritual weapons, and the most powerful is prayer."

Nate turned around and smiled down at her. "How did you get so smart about all things spiritual?"

Faith's Legacy

Charlie snorted at his question. "You've met my parents, right?" she replied with a grin. "I was raised and trained for spiritual battles the same way you were trained for combat in the East. I may not have all the answers, but one thing I know how to do is pray."

I've always admired the strength of your family's faith, even when I didn't understand it. I wish I had been raised the way you were."

Charlie shook her head as they both sat down on the side of the bed. "It wasn't always easy, especially in my teen years. All I wanted was a 'normal' family. I didn't want to have to worry that if I brought a friend home would we walk into a prayer session or a Bible study. I wanted to be able to go and do all the things that my friends could do, but so often I couldn't because Mama wouldn't have 'peace' about it. I really started to resent that word, but you know what?"

"What?"

"I want to raise our children the exact same way. I want to have the Lord's help and guidance like my mama did. One of her favorite things to do when I argued about wanting to do something that she didn't want me to do was to tell me to go pray about it."

"And would you?" Nate asked.

Charlie nodded, "Oh, yes, I would, and every single time I would get the same feeling that Mama had been talking about." She stopped and laughed as she recalled her childhood. "I would go back and tell her that God was always on her side, and it wasn't fair."

"What would she say?"

"She told me that it was the other way around. She was on God's side and that she hoped and prayed that I would always be on his side, too."

"It looks like her prayers were answered. You are a strong woman of faith just like her."

Charlie raised her eyes to his. "No, I'm nothing like my mama. It seems as if she has a direct line straight to heaven. One day maybe I will be more like her but I'm not there yet. I think you have to go through some things to obtain the kind of faith that she has."

Nate reached out and cupped Charlie's chin, bringing her face close to his. "I think it's not about matching your mom's faith. God has a road mapped out just for you, and your faith will be based on you and Him walking that road together." He kissed the tip of her nose.

Charlie smiled. "I think you're right. Everyone's faith is different. It's not about more or less. It's a personal thing. My relationship with the Lord will never be exactly like my mama's because that's hers."

Nate nodded. "That's it." He sighed as he ran his hands over his face. He no longer cringed when his fingertips brushed over the uneven tissue of his scars. He knew they were there but he refused to let them define him any longer. He often wondered if Charlie even saw them anymore. She looked at him like she did before he was wounded. In a way, that helped him to forget them, too.

"We need to find a way to be at the hospital more."

Nate glanced up, brought out of his private musings by Charlie's statement. "How do you mean?"

"Well, I think we need to be close by to keep it guarded with prayer and…" she trailed off when Nate jumped to his feet.

"That's it! That's how we can help!" he said in a near shout.

"Umm…that's what we have been saying all along. Why all the excitement now?"

"Because the word you said triggered something in me. Guard…we can guard the hospital with prayer. Guarding is something I know how to do." He started pacing the floor, his brow deeply wrinkled as he thought out his plan.

"We need more prayer warriors." He lifted his hand to stop her when Charlie opened her mouth to point out that her parents were praying. "I mean we need more local prayer warriors, the ones that can be here with us and help us to provide a visible shield of protection around the hospital. Let the enemy know that we are on to him."

"But where can we find more people? We don't] here."

Nate smiled when Mac shimmered into view. "Don't worry, babe; the Lord will always provide."

Mac and Shana flew quickly through the night skies over the state of California. They were on a scouting mission looking for spirit-filled prayer warriors. Since Nate and Charlie were sleeping and not likely to go anywhere for a few hours, Gideon stayed behind to watch over them so Mac and Shana could go find some help.

"How will we know where to find them?" Shana asked as they dropped lower, barely missing the rooftops.

"I can smell it," Mac replied as he wrinkled his nose and sniffed deeply like a bloodhound on the trail of his prey. He all but threw back his head and howled.

"Smell it? Are you serious?" Shana asked with a grin and a shake of her head at Mac's antics.

"Of course, I'm serious. All prayers have a distinct smell," he pointed out.

"They do not -- I have never smelled a prayer!" she argued.

Mac gave her a lop-sided grin. "Maybe you have. You just didn't know what you were smelling."

"Ok, fine. What does a prayer smell like?"

"Depends."

"On what?"

"What kind of prayer it is."   When Shana growled at him, he laughed. "Okay, okay...I will explain. Now to me prayers all have the scent of flowers. Some, like prayers for healing, have a soothing scent of jasmine; prayers for wisdom smell like lilies; but strong faith-filled prayers smell like gardenias."

Shana looked at Mac so surprised that she nearly forgot to keep moving her wings to stay in the air. "Oh! I have smelled that! On Sabrina! I just thought it was the scent of the soap she used or something, but she always smells like gardenias.".

Mac nodded. "Yup, I told you. So, now that you know what smell we are looking for, keep that nose of yours in the wind!"

An hour later Shana caught a faint whiff of gardenia and raised her hand to get Mac's attention. He nodded to let her know he smelled it, too.

They searched the area, closing in on the scent, and tracked it to an unlikely spot. A small hut just off the beach seemed to be the source of the prayer. As they touched down on the soft sand, the music of The Beach Boys was blended with a rhythmic, scraping sound. They walked in to find a man somewhere between the age of twenty-five and thirty-five working on a surfboard. His long light brown hair was streaked with copper from hours in the sun and his skin was tanned a deep shade of a true Californian. Wearing nothing but ragged cut-off shorts, he worked at shaping a new surf board as he kept up a steady conversation with God, pausing to sing along with the song occasionally.

"Oh, wow..." Shana said as she hid her grin behind her hand.

Mac chuckled. "Yeah, this is great! I can't wait for Nate to meet this guy. California surfer meets Carolina redneck. This is going to be epic!"

Chapter 3

Two days later Nate was sitting in the front lobby of the hospital; he had chosen this as his post. He would hang out and visit with people as they came in while praying protection over the hospital. Charlie had decided to stay in waiting rooms on different floors. She said the Lord would lead her to what floor she needed to be on. Dr. Reed agreed that something needed to be done. While still a new Christian, he had believed in the power of prayer even before he committed his life to Christ. He told them they were more than welcome to stay and pray over the hospital if no one complained about them being there. He desperately needed something to stop all the patients from coding. He admitted to not understanding all the workings of spiritual warfare, but he was willing to learn. Hattie, on the other hand, knew about the spiritual side of things, so she readily agreed to Nate and Charlie's creating a "prayer guard."

When the man walked in, Nate noticed him right away. He was the picture of a California surfer with long sun-streaked hair, board shorts and a t-shirt with a large wooden cross on a string around his neck; he was hard to miss. He paused in the lobby, searching the room with his light green eyes. His gazed rested on Nate for a moment then moved on only to swing right back to him.

He smiled as he approached, holding out his hand. "Hey, dude, I'm Brody, and I think you're the one I was sent here to talk to."

Nate looked up in surprise. "I'm Nate Jackson. I don't really know too many people here. Are you sure I'm the one you're looking for?"

"For sure, dude, I was sent to this hospital and told to look for the soldier. I'm guessing from all your war wounds that would be you, bro."

"I was in the military," Nate confirmed. "So, who sent you?"

Brody pointed upward. "The Big Papa in the sky, bro. He told me that you needed some serious help. So, I'm here to offer my services."

Faith's Legacy

Nate's gaze slid over to Mac, who was grinning at him wildly. "Trust me, he is the one you need. Fill him in on everything that is going on," he assured.

Nate nodded. "Okay then, Brody, I would like for you to meet my wife. She is upstairs. After we do that, I will fill you in on what we believe to be happening here."

Gideon's eyes widened when Nate and Brody, followed by Mac and Shana, stepped off the elevator. Charlie was visiting with a patient's family member, so he had stepped out of the room to patrol the hallway.

Gideon asked the obvious with the lift of his brow. Mac grinned in response. "Trust me -- he is exactly what we need."

When Gideon looked at Shana, she nodded in agreement. "He had the strongest scent for miles."

"Scent? Oh, you mean the scent of his prayers. Was it gardenias?"

Shana's frown looked more like a cute little pout as she tossed her hands up into the air. "Am I the only one who didn't know about the scent of prayers?"

Gideon and Mac looked at her then each other and shrugged. "I don't know, but we won't tell if you don't," Mac offered with a wink.

Gideon stood studying the man that Mac had so much faith in. To look at him he didn't look like someone who would smell strongly of gardenias, but he couldn't deny the powerful fragrance that surrounded him. One thing he had learned while guarding Charlie was you really could not judge a human by appearance.

Charlie looked up when Nate and another man walked up to her. Smiling, she excused herself from the woman she had just been praying with then stood up to meet them.

"Brody, this is my wife of almost two weeks, Charlie. Charlie, this is Brody. He was sent to help us with our 'situation,'" he said, using air quotes.

Brody inclined his head in greeting. "Pleased to meet you. Looks like Nate scored a massive A-Frame with you, love." Slugging Nate lightly on the shoulder, he leaned in and whispered, "She's a keeper, bro. Gorgeous inside and out, you know?"

Charlie's cheeks turned a shade pinker. Although she didn't understand what an "A-Frame" was, she felt that Brody meant the term as a compliment.

"Hi, I'm happy to meet you, too. I'm especially happy that you are here to help."

"No, prob. When the big Kahuna tells me to go, I go. Why don't we go somewhere where we can speak freely?" Giving the other people in the room a swift glance, they understood what he was saying.

"Sure, how about we go back to our hotel room and order some pizza? It's getting to be supper time soon and I, for one, am starving!" Charlie suggested.

"I'm totally down for some pizza, little lady dude. But only if I buy." Brody held up his hands when both Nate and Charlie started to protest. "Hey, no harshness! It's just the way I roll, okay?" Once they understood that Brody wasn't going to change his mind, Nate and Charlie agreed, after promising they would buy next time.

Once they headed out of the hospital, Gideon fell into step next to Mac. "I hope you can translate, because I only understood about every third word that came out of his mouth."

Mac snorted as he clapped a hand across Gideon's broad shoulder. "No worries, old man. I got ya!"

Gideon shook his head. "That's cute, considering we are *exactly*, the same age."

"Yeah, but I got a young soul!" Mac said with a wink.

Once everyone had reached the hotel and had eaten their fill of pizza, Brody stood up and walked over to the window.

"I think we should start this meeting with prayer. I never start anything without asking for the Lord's lead." Without waiting for anyone's agreement, Brody dropped his head.

"Father God, we ask for you to lead us in the direction that we should go. We ask that you bring the right people to help us fight the big evil that is trying to take over. I pray for your protection and that you send your biggest angels to help us defeat the enemy."

Faith's Legacy

Once he had finished, he sat down and for once the playful look was gone from his green eyes. He was all business.

"Tell me what's going on."

Nate started from the beginning. "I was seriously injured in a helicopter accident while I was enlisted. I was sent to Southern California Trauma Unit. After I recovered and Charlie and I were married, we returned because I wanted to show her more of California and I wanted her to meet some of the friends that I had made. While we were visiting the hospital, patients were coding left and right, one right after another. Dr. Reed, who was my doctor, told us that they had been having an unusual number of patients coding and dying. I believe that the hospital is under some sort of demonic attack. Now I'm not sure where you stand as far as demons are concerned…"

"I stand right on their necks like the Bible tells me to do," Brody interjected with a fierce expression. "I don't tolerate the evil things. Jesus didn't give them any slack and I don't either."

"Have you ever dealt with anything like this before?" Charlie asked.

Brody rubbed the back of neck as he answered. "I have but it isn't something that I go looking for. First thing, we need to find out just what 'This' is. The fact that you were here before and this wasn't happening means something either has changed or is going to change and the enemy doesn't like it. But I know we can handle it."

"You sound pretty sure of yourself," Nate commented.

Brody flashed a smile at him. "Nah, bro. Not me. I'm real sure about WHO I serve."

Mac nudged Gideon's shoulder with a grin on his face. "See? What did I tell you? He is perfect."

Gideon rubbed his jaw as he considered the man that was visiting with Nate and Charlie. "He does seem to have a lot of faith, which is good. We will need all that we can get."

For next few hours the three humans discussed various plans and counter plans to cleanse the hospital of the darkness that was intent on taking over.

A small demon of doubt and disbelief flew as fast as his little membrane wings would carry him. He must reach Karau and tell him what he had just seen and heard.

"He will not be pleased... not pleased at all," he moaned. Dread filled his mind and he wished he could keep silent about what he saw. Swooping down through the dark earth, he sped quickly past roots, boulders and soil until he flew into the open space of the cavern that was located under the hospital. Karau was surrounded by larger and stronger demons that all sneered in disgust as he dropped to the floor, allowing his wings to drag behind him as he carefully approached.

"Lord Karau, I beg your attention for a moment, sir."

Karau turned to the little demon that was crawling on the floor making his way toward him while being kicked and spat upon by the others in the room.

"What do you want?" he asked.

"Sir, I...I have news to...to report. Important news!" The little demon was so nervous he could barely form the words he needed.

"Well, what are you waiting for? Tell me what you know," Karau demanded in a deceptively-soft voice.

"Sir, I saw those humans, the ones that are always with Gideon. I saw them tonight with a man of great faith. They are making plans to cleanse the hospital!" He wrung his clawed fingers as he waited to see what his master would say.

Karau lifted his right brow slightly. "And?" he prompted.

He lifted his head slightly, beady red eyes darted around the room as if someone might offer him some assistance. Of course, no one did.

"I...I... have nothing else, but I thought you would want to know."

Karau took three steps and without warning he viciously kicked the small demon, sending him flying across the cavern where he slammed into the wall. Karau walked over to where he lay on the floor wheezing, trying to breathe through the pain of his shattered ribs. Karau calmly gazed down at him with no emotion.

"Do you think I am unaware of things happening in my territory? Do you think I fear this Gideon whom I have already had swinging at the end of my rope?" Walking slowly around the room, he looked in the eye of each minion who was present.

"Mark my words, he will be there again, and this time there will be no rescue."

Charlie took the hands of the young woman named Amy sitting next to her in the hospital waiting room. She knew all too well the hopeless feeling the young lady had just expressed.

"You must keep believing for your miracle. I know that from where you sit right now it seems pointless, but take it from me -- where there is faith, there is always hope."

Amy shook her head as tears escaped down her face. "I'm not strong like you are, Miss Charlie. I try to pray, but the words just get stuck in my throat and won't come out. I'm not even sure if I'm praying the right way."

Charlie leaned in closer until she was mere inches from the woman's face. "As long as you're praying, then you're doing it right. Keep talking to God. Tell him exactly how you feel. If you're scared, then tell him; if you're angry, then tell him that, too. The point is to keep the line of communication open."

Gray eyes searched Charlie's face as if all her answers could be found there.

"What if Chance dies? What if I pray exactly all the right things and he dies anyway?"

Pulling her into her arms, Charlie hugged her tightly. "That's when you pray even harder. I don't know what God's answer will be, Amy. I'm sorry. But I do know that he will do what is best for Chance. Sometimes God heals them here on earth and sometimes he brings them home to heal them."

"I can't live without him... I can't... You don't understand!" Pulling away, she ran from the room, leaving Charlie staring after her.

Faith's Legacy

Once Amy was in the hallway, a demon of fear jumped onto the girl's shoulders, stroking his clawed fingers gently over her hair as he whispered into her ear: "He won't live...You will be alone... He won't live... You will be alone." Over and over he repeated his poisoned words until they penetrated deep into her heart...

Charlie's heart was so burdened by Amy's situation. Like Nate, her husband Chance had been seriously wounded and his survival wasn't certain. She knew there were others, so many others who were in the same boat. Closing her eyes, she sought out her peace, focusing on the scripture found in John 14:27: "Peace I leave with you, My peace I give to you; not as the world gives do I give to you. Let not your heart be troubled, neither let it be afraid. "

"My heavenly Father, I seek your peace during this time. I also seek your wisdom and your guidance. Show me how to help your children who are so frightened." Charlie paused as a picture popped into her head almost like a memory. It was an image of the waiting room she was standing in, but this time it was filled with people holding hands and praying together. Surrounding the circle of people, she saw evil lurking in the shadows, but standing between them and the darkness was a brilliant light, a hedge of protection. Within this hedge, she could just make out the glint of silver swords and the arch of angel wings.

Charlie lifted her head with a gasp. "I know what to do!"

Gideon followed Charlie closely as she walked quickly out of the waiting room and into the hallway. He couldn't see the evil that was waiting there, but he certainly could feel it. Every feather he had bristled and tingled, stopping just short of turning into sharp weapons. Since Charlie had started praying with people in the waiting area, she had driven out any demons from the room, but they didn't go far. He knew they were looking for the ones they could attack. Walking behind her, he spread open his wings slightly to form a wall to shield her.

Charlie rushed into the front lobby, where Nate and Brody were talking to an older gentleman. She slid to a stop next to Nate, who smiled at her excited expression.

"Hi, there. Looks like you have something important to say," he teased.

"Uhh…, yes, I do but it can wait until you have finished visiting with your friend," she replied as she smiled at the stranger.

"Charlie, this is my friend, Pastor Tony Pauline. He officiates at Hope for the Lost Ministries on Pinewood Street."

"Hi, it's great to meet you. I love the name of your church!" she said with a smile.

Pastor Tony was a man just past middle age with a slight paunch to his belly. His thick head of hair was more gray than black, but the fire that glowed inside him lit up his face. "Why, thank you, my dear girl. It wasn't a hard name to come up with, for isn't that exactly what Jesus is? Hope for all lost souls?"

"Yes, sir, he certainly is," Charlie agreed.

"I was just filling Pastor Tony in on some of the activities at the hospital. He said that the Lord showed him a vision." Brody nodded at the pastor. "Go ahead and tell Nate and Charlie what you told me."

"Okay, it was while I was having my prayer time, just this morning. I saw myself in a room with a group of people that I did not know. We were all holding hands and praying together in a circle. Just outside the circle I saw a ring of white light filled with angels, and beyond the angels were devils trying to break through to get to us, but the angels of the Lord held them back!" He finished his story with a wide smile.

Charlie felt the blood drain from her face while goosebumps raced across her skin. Nate noticed and asked if she was all right.

She looked up at the three men standing there as she licked her suddenly-dry lips nervously. "Ummm… that's what I came down here to tell you, I just had that same exact vision upstairs. Pastor Tony, I think I know where the room is that you saw in your vision."

Faith's Legacy

A few minutes later they all stood in the waiting room on the 7th floor. "Is this the room you saw, Pastor?" Charlie asked.

After looking carefully, he nodded. "Yes! Yes, I'm sure this is it!" he turned to Charlie, grasping her hands gently. "You see, my dear girl, the Lord will always confirm his plans through two or more of his children. By giving you and me the same vision, this is how we know for certain that we are in the will of God."

"So, what were you doing in this vision? Just praying?" Nate asked.

"Pastor Tony looked at Nate with a serious expression. "No, son. We were not just praying. We were going to battle!" He then gave Charlie a serious look, "And this young lady was leading the charge."

Chapter 4

Charlie looked at Pastor Tony with a stunned expression. "Me? I don't know anything about leading something like this. When I had the vision, I didn't see me leading anything. I was just there."

"That's because you couldn't see yourself and the role you would play. I saw you clearly and you were calm and knowledgeable and in charge."

When Charlie opened her mouth to protest further, Pastor Tony shook his head. "I know what you're going to say. But God has sent me to prepare you for whatever it is that is going to happen. Fear not, my child."

"Whoa…dude, that is extremely awesome," Brody said as he aimed a wide smile at Charlie.

"I can feel a great power flowing from this man," Gideon commented to Shana as they stood by quietly listening. "He reminds me of someone I met a long time ago."

"Who was it?" Shana asked.

"King David. He was a man who made many mistakes but never lost his love for God."

Shana cocked her head slightly, looking over the non-descript pastor. "What did you do for King David?"

Gideon grinned. "Let's just say he had a little help when he stood against Goliath."

"So, he didn't kill him with a stone from his sling?"

"Oh, yes, he did, without a doubt. He had great courage and he flung that stone straight and true. I just added a little extra oomph behind it."

Seeing the questions burning in her eyes, Gideon knew he would have to tell her the entire story…

"So, you remember the basic story of David and Goliath, right? Shepard boy kills giant Philistine with a rock and sling?" Gideon paused to give Shana time to reply.

"Isn't that what happened?"

"Yes, but what I'm going to tell you in the back story, or maybe the behind-the- scenes story would be more accurate. I had a

Faith's Legacy

large troupe of warriors camped out in the valley Philistines were camped on one side and the Israel other. The surrounding areas were filled black with legions of demon fiends. The air was heavy and stan... ne enemy was heavily influencing the Philistines, and the Israelites were sorely lacking in faith. We were there to keep things somewhat in check although, to be honest, I had no clue what was about to happen, or what we could do if something did happen. Without faith-filled prayers, we were pretty lacking in the strength department. I knew that our Creator always has a remnant, but none of the men there had the faith needed to defeat Goliath. So, one day this young boy shows up to see his brothers, and from the moment he stepped into view, I could tell he was something special."

"How so? What was so special about a young shepherd boy?"

"Hang on, hold your horses -- I'm getting to that point," Gideon said with a mock frown.

"Sorry...sorry...continue," Shana said with an eager grin.

"Now, like I said, as soon I saw David approaching the camps, I could see he was special. A glow surrounded him. It was faint, but it was there. I knew I needed to keep an eye on this one. Sure enough, not long after he arrived, Old Goliath started in with his teasing and taunting of the Israelites and David heard him. The look on his face was priceless! He was beyond furious and he honestly did not understand why no one was standing up to this bully. His brothers all tried to hush him up, but David wasn't having it. Word finally got back to Saul that there was someone who was willing to face the giant, and his eyes nearly popped out of his head when he saw David. This young boy barely old enough to tend sheep alone was willing to face the champion of the Philistine army? Saul questioned David, asking him why he thought he could defeat Goliath. Here is the part I will never forget: David looked King Saul straight in the eye and told him that if God would give him strength to defeat the lions and the bears, then he would give him strength to defeat the enemy of Israel. I had my men gather close around this young man because I knew that was our remnant."

Faith's Legacy

"Wow… out of all the people it was only young David who had the faith to stand up and say, 'No more!' So, what happened then?" Shana had, of course, heard this famous story, but to hear it the way Gideon was telling it made it come to life for her.

"Saul tried to get David to wear his armor, but the poor kid could hardly stand up under the weight of all of it. Kept toppling over every time he tried to move." Gideon chuckled at the memory. "So, he took it all off, thanked Saul politely and then went out and picked up some stones. Walking across the open area between the camps, he called out to Goliath. Of course, the giant was amused and somewhat insulted that this little whelp would dare to go up against him. A hush fell across the valley when David boldly told him that he came in the name of the Lord. I stepped up next to him and just before he slipped the stone into the sling and let it fly, I reached out, grabbed his wrist, adding my strength to his. The stone nailed the giant right between the eyes, hitting him so hard that it sank deeply into his forehead, killing him instantly."

"After that the Israelites tore into the Philistines, who saw that their champion had been defeated by a mere shepherd boy. They lost all their muster and fled. My warriors wasted little time clearing the valley of evil that day."

"I had no idea that we helped in that battle, at least not in that way," Shana said with a smile.

"Most don't, but the moral of that story is this: If you have the faith and the courage to step up and face your giants, no matter what they may be, God will always back you up. I can see the same faint glow around Pastor Tony that I saw around David, so you can bet I will be keeping my eye on that one!"

Later that night Nate pulled Charlie into his arms after they had turned off the lights and gone to bed. "I'm sorry, babe. I know this isn't the honeymoon that most women dream about."

Charlie lifted her head. The moonlight coming through the open curtains illuminated his face, showing the frown that was creasing his forehead.

"Hey, you don't hear me complaining, do you?" she whispered as she placed baby kisses along his jawline.

"No, and I know that you wouldn't, but I just wanted you to know that I didn't bring you to California expecting to be involved in whatever it is that we are involved in."

"I know that! How could you know? I'm just glad that we are here to help, although what Pastor Tony said has me a little concerned," she admitted with a sigh.

"About you being a leader? Why does that concern you? I can totally see that in you."

"You can?" Charlie asked in surprise.

"Of course, and I think under Pastor Tony there is no telling what you are capable of."

"I don't know, Nate. I don't feel much like a leader. There is still so much that I don't know or understand," Charlie said as she laid her head on Nate's shoulder.

"If God has called you to do something, then he will make sure you're ready. Your job is to just be willing."

Charlie grinned as she rose up and kissed him. "You are sounding pretty wise, Mr. Jackson."

"Why, thank you, Mrs. Jackson. I always aim to impress."

Hattie entered Chance Miller's room. The steady beep of the heart monitor and the even hiss of the ventilator were the only sounds in the dimly-lit room. Placing her hand on his chest, she closed her eyes to say a prayer of healing over the young man.

"I'm sure they didn't teach you that nonsense in nursing school."

Hattie jumped then scowled at the dark corner of the room where the voice came from. "Actually, they taught us that whatever brings the patients peace was encouraged," she replied as she squinted her eyes to see who was standing in the darkness.

"Hmmm... peace, is that what they are calling it these days?" The voice had an almost-disgusted tone.

"Who are you? Why are you in this room?" Hattie demanded as she walked over and flipped on the light. A gasp of shock left her lips as she raised her hand to her suddenly-racing heart. The room was empty except for Chance and herself; there was no one else.

Hattie opened the door and rushed out into the hall only to run smack into Dr. Reed. He grabbed her shoulders to steady her, looking at her with concern.

"Why, Hattie, you're as white as a sheet! Are you okay?"

"No, Doctor, I don't think I am," she replied as she took a few steps away from the door.

"Is it the patient?" he asked as he opened the door and peeked inside.

"No, sir, the patient is fine. It's my own sanity that I'm questioning now."

"Why don't we step into this waiting room and you can sit down and tell me what happened."

After Hattie had sat down, Dr. Reed handed her a cup of water. She took a long swallow and let out a deep breath. "I'm warning you -- this sounds crazy, but I swear it happened." After Dr. Reed nodded his head, she continued. "I had gone in to check on the patient and while I was there I was going to say a little prayer for healing, like I usually do. But when I placed my hand on his chest, I heard someone speak from the corner of the room. He asked if nursing schools taught that nonsense. I replied that they taught us to do whatever brought the patients peace. It then replied, 'Hmmm...peace, is that what they call it these days?'" Hattie stood up and walked across the room to toss the empty cup into the wastebasket. She did it more to expel the nervous energy she was feeling than any real concern about keeping the room tidy.

"So, who was it that spoke to you? Have you seen him here before?"

Hattie snorted slightly, "You see, Doctor, that's the problem. I didn't turn on any lights when I entered, being that I was only doing a quick check on the patient, so the only light came from the bedside monitor. When I turned on the light to see who was speaking," she paused and looked the doctor straight in the eye, "there was no one there." Hattie watched Dr. Reed closely, knowing he was going to send her home for being nuts.

She took it as a good sign that he didn't laugh in her face but seemed to be considering what she had told him. "I'm assuming you're positive it wasn't the patient speaking?" he asked.

Hattie vehemently shook her head. "No, sir! The voice came from the other side of the room. I was standing right next to the patient with my hand on his chest. He never moved nor did his breathing change, which it would have if it had been him that had spoken."

"No chance that the speaker left the room before you turned on the light?"

Again, Hattie shook her head. "Not possible. I would have seen the door open and I would have seen whoever it was leave the room." Hattie sat back down next to the doctor and gave him a small smile. "I understand if you want me to go home for the night or forever. I know I sound crazy."

Dr. Reed covered her hand with his, giving it a gentle squeeze. "You are the best nurse I have ever worked with. I know that you are, without a doubt, of sound mind. You sound confused right now, not crazy, and who wouldn't be after experiencing such an odd thing? Now if you would like to go home, I have no problem with that, but I'm not sending you home. I don't know what happened in that room tonight, but I believe every word you said, and I think we need to make sure that Nate and Charlie know about it as well."

"I will tell them first thing in the morning. They usually arrive before I'm off duty." She rubbed the back of her neck wearily.

"Hey, we will figure this out, okay? Would you like to pray together right now?" he offered.

"Yes...yes, I would!"

Together they each took turns praying for peace for Hattie's troubled heart and mind, for wisdom to know how to handle the situation, and lastly, they prayed for the safety of all the patients who were in their care.

"So why are you here so late?" Hattie asked after they had left the waiting room and were heading back to the nurse's station.

"I can't relax at home worrying about all the problems we are having here. How's it been tonight?" Concern had etched itself deeply on the good doctor's face. Hattie noticed that the gray at his temples was becoming thicker.

"We had one code but were able to stabilize the patient."

They both stopped at the nurse's station. Shelia, one of the other night nurses, was sitting at the desk charting; she smiled as they walked up.

"Good evening, doctor. Why are you here so late?" she asked.

"Hello, Shelia, I just dropped in to check on a few patients. Can I ask you a question? It may seem," he paused then shook his head, "no, it most definitely will seem odd, but have you encountered anything strange while tending to the patients?"

The nurse frowned slightly, "Strange? What do you mean?"

"Like hearing someone speak to you but when you turn on the light there isn't anyone there, strange," Hattie said.

A guarded look quickly crossed the nurse's face, before she looked down at the desk.

"Shelia?" Dr. Reed prompted.

"Well, I wasn't going to say anything…but there was something that happened last night that spooked me a little." She looked up with a self-mocking smile. "I'm *sure* it was just my imagination. You know, one too many horror movies coming back to haunt me." She laughed slightly before continuing. "I had been making my rounds and everything was fine until I went into room 334. When I opened the door, I thought just for a moment that I saw something in the room with the patient."

"Some*thing*? Not someone?" Hattie questioned.

Sheila rubbed at her temples a second before shaking her head. "Not a someone, Miss Hattie. What I saw wasn't human."

"Can you describe it?" Dr. Reed asked her as he looked up and down the hallway.

"It was tall...extremely tall. Well over seven feet, if I had to guess, and it was oddly shaped. Its arms and legs were long and very thin while its torso was short and compact. But it was the head that scared me to death." She paused as a shudder went through her. "It had a head like a T-Rex...oblong-shaped with a huge mouth and lots and lots of teeth."

Dr. Reed and Hattie shared a long glance. "What was it doing when you saw it?" he asked.

"It looked like it was sticking its long talons into the patient's chest. When I opened the door, it turned its head, stared at me for a second then disappeared. I only saw it for maybe ten or twelve seconds, but it seemed so solid and real. I have tried to figure out if maybe I was seeing an odd shadow or if my eyes were playing tricks on me or something."

"How was the patient reacting? Was he showing signs of distress?" the doctor asked with a look of concern on his face.

"Yes, he was moaning slightly. After I got my nerve up to go on into the room, I checked his vitals and I saw that he had a sudden drop in blood pressure."

"How much did it drop? What was it; do you recall?"

"It dropped a lot, down to 66/45 from 117/78. I honestly think if I hadn't walked in on it that the patient would have coded."

Dr. Reed smacked his palm on the desktop. "That's what making all our patients code on us! We have to figure out what it is and how to get rid of it."

"This can't be happening. It's like something from a science fiction movie!" Sheila said in disbelief as she looked from Dr. Reed to Hattie.

"What do you think? What does your gut tell you?" Hattie asked as she came around the desk and wrapped a comforting arm around the woman's shoulders.

Sheila closed her eyes for a moment as she thought about Hattie's question. Finally, she nodded as she made up her mind. "I saw what I saw, as crazy as it sounds. It *was* dark in the room, but there was enough light from the hallway when I opened the door for me to see it clearly. I won't ever forget it."

Dr. Reed gave the nurse a reassuring smile. "Thank you for sharing that. I think we need to speak to others and see if anyone else has had similar encounters."

"So, you do believe me?" Shelia asked with a surprised look.

"Yes, I believe you saw something; I just need to find out exactly what it was you saw. If something else happens, anything at all, please tell myself or Nurse Hattie."

"Yes, sir. I sure will."

During the next hour, they spoke to four more nurses. Three had nothing to report, but one admitted to seeing the same creature that Shelia had described.

"Well, I guess the silver lining in all of this is if I'm crazy, at least I'm not alone in my insanity," Hattie said with a sigh as she and Dr. Reed made their way to the rear of the hospital to the underground garage. Standing in the doorway of the garage, Dr. Reed rubbed his tired eyes.

"I don't know what to make of any of this, to be honest. I guess I have always known there was a flip side to the coin of good and evil, but I never had any reason to study it," he admitted with a sigh.

"We have a reason now, wouldn't you say?" Hattie replied before bidding him a good night.

Chapter 5

A few hours later a frazzled Hattie gave Nate and Charlie a happy but tired smile when they arrived at the hospital.

"I'm sure glad to see you two!"

Nate gave the woman a quick hug. "It's always great to see you, too, but I get the feeling that it's more than just my handsome face that has you so eager to see us."

Patting Nate's jaw affectionately, she smiled at her favorite former patient. "This morning I'm afraid it is more than that face of yours. I'm afraid we have had a very interesting night and not in a good way." Looking around she motioned for them to follow her into an unoccupied room and told them everything that had happened the night before.

Charlie looked at Hattie with eyes as round as saucers.

"Oh, Hattie! You must have been terrified!"

"I think I was too confused to be frightened when it happened. It wasn't until later when I finally decided I wasn't crazy that I got really spooked. Then hearing the other nurses' stories didn't help any. So, what do we do?" Hattie looked at Nate and then Charlie expectantly.

"I don't know, but if you can give us a few hours we will try to find out. Go home and get some rest. You look exhausted," Nate commented as he took in her tired eyes and slumped shoulders.

"I think I will. I am tired. My shift is over in just a few more minutes. I will keep my cell phone on today, so please call me if anything else happens or if you find out what the devil we are dealing with."

"You just called it by its name, Hattie. The devil is exactly what we are dealing with and we are going to show him the door just as soon as possible!" Nate replied with a determined look.

"You know it's allowing itself to be seen, right?"

Mac nodded at Gideon's comment. "Yes, I don't know as much about demonic warfare as you do, but I do know they don't show their hand unless it's for a reason. It could be for the fear factor alone or something else."

"Fear can be very hindering, and it gives them something to feed on. So, what do we do?" Shana asked.

Gideon placed a hand on Shana's shoulder. "We cut off their food supply by fighting fear with faith."

Mac's grin spread across his face. "Are you thinking what I'm thinking?" he asked.

Gideon nodded. "It's time to call in the troops!"

Down the hall, Nate saw Mac motion that he needed to speak to him in private. He nodded slightly to let him know he got the message then a couple minutes later excused himself to go to the restroom. The one on this hall was a single use restroom, so it was perfect as long he kept his voice down while speaking. Once inside, he turned on the faucet to drown out his voice.

"I know you heard everything Hattie said, so what's the plan?" he asked.

"The plan is we get Charlie's family up here ASAP. We need the power of their prayers and their faith to combat the fear that this thing is creating in people."

"That shouldn't be a problem. Do we know what this is and why it's happening?"

Mac shook his head. "No, we haven't got it all figured out yet, but when her family arrives, we will have more heads in the game."

"Can't you recruit some local angels or something in the meantime? It will most likely be a few days before they can all get here. I'm assuming you want all of them, right?"

"I'm going to do that after I finish talking to you, and yes, have everyone who can come get on a plane as quickly as possible. I will let you know more as I know more, and Nate?"

"What?"

"Stay in constant prayer. I have a feeling we are just seeing the tip of the iceberg."

Charlie saw Amy come out of her husband's room looking pale and worn down. Hurrying over to her, she gave her a smile.

"Amy, hi, how's he doing?"

The young woman shook her head as she wiped away a tear. "Not good, Charlie. Not good at all. The doctor said it's all in God's hands now, that there isn't anything more that they can do for him medically."

Charlie grasped Amy's hands tightly. "Then Chance is exactly where he needs to be...in God's loving hands. This where we must stand in faith. Remember me telling you that faith the size of a mustard seed can move mountains?"

Amy gave Charlie a small, sad smile. "I don't think I even have that small amount right now, to be honest."

"Then I will loan you some of mine. I know what God can do. I have seen it with my own eyes. They said the same thing about Nate and you have seen him yourself, so you know miracles can happen."

"I don't know; I don't have the faith that you do. It might not happen for us."

"Amy, listen to me. God is no respecter of people. What he did for me he will do for you. Do you think I didn't have moments of weakness or being scared out of my mind?"

Amy's gray eyes searched Charlie's face. "Did you really? I have a hard time believing that. You seem so strong."

"Everyone has their moments of doubt and fear, even the strongest of believers. When you are too weak, that's when someone else carries you on the strength of their faith until you can stand again. I will carry you. I will pray when you can't find the words to say. I will fall on my knees until you can fall to yours. You are never ever alone; do you hear me?"

Amy nodded as tears streamed down her face. Reaching out, she fell into Charlie's arms, clinging to her like a person lost at sea might cling to a life raft.

Charlie held Amy tightly as she rocked and prayed, trying to will some of her faith into Amy's trembling body. She felt Nate walk up beside them, and without a word he wrapped strong arms around them both, adding his faith to Charlie's. What they couldn't see was the demon of fear being thrown off the young woman's shoulders. A golden glow surrounded the three of them. As Charlie and Nate called out to the ONE they knew could deliver Amy's husband, an explosion of faith lit up the hospital waiting room and sent showers of light throughout the hospital.

Down the hall, the demon of disease felt a searing pain in his left leg. Looking down, he saw a shaft of pure white light protruding from his thigh. Before he had time to react, another shaft of light pierced through his cloud of darkness, entering his body just below his left shoulder. Emitting a scream of pain and rage, he dropped through the floor, escaping before any more arrows found their mark.

Mac smiled as he watched the wounded demon flee. "That's right; go tell your leader that if he wants a battle, he just found one!"

Sabrina set the cell phone on the table and turned to Devon, who was there with her. "What on earth do you think is going on at that hospital?" she asked with a frown.

"I don't know, babe, but it's bad enough that they are calling in help. Do you want to call your folks? I can call Cleo and see if her crew can make the trip."

Sabrina clapped her hands in delight. "Cleo! Of course, I hope she can come. Those nasty old things are in for a very unpleasant surprise."

Charlotte grinned at Zareck, who had taken out his sword and was running a sandstone slowly over the edges.

"Looks like we are going to California!" she said with an excited clap.

Zareck gave her a quick wink. "Yes, it sounds as if Gideon has found trouble. We better go save him."

Charlotte snorted. "I'm so telling him you said that!"

Zareck smiled. "I'm *so* hoping you do."

"I can't wait to see Kavik again. It will be like old times with all of us back together." Charlotte did a happy little dance step then reached over and pulled Zareck up, making him twirl around the room with her.

"Dude… you are so light on your feet!" Skye teased from the staircase.

"Better watch your toes, Charlotte!" Raphael chimed in.

Zareck just laughed as he gracefully waltzed Charlotte around the living room without missing a step or stepping on any bare toes!

Down in south Louisiana:
Kavik watched the expression on Cleo's face change from happy, to concerned to determined, as Devon explained what was happening in California.

"Oh, that poor baby. You tell Charlie girl that her Cleo will be there just as soon as I can make arrangements, but in the meantime, you can be sure I will be praying! Yes, sir, I will be there as soon as I can."

Kavik heard perfectly every word Devon said over the phone and knew without a doubt that they would soon be making a trip to the Golden State. Reaching back, he pulled one dark gray wing over his shoulder, running his fingers through the downy soft feathers. He still couldn't believe that his wings had grown back, and he couldn't wait to show his friends.

Cleo paced the floor of her living room, praying power and protection over Charlie and Nate and the entire hospital, when she suddenly stopped and reached for her phone. A few minutes later she placed the phone back in its cradle. She stomped her foot and shook her fist in the air.

"That's right, you old devil! You better hear me now...because we are coming for ya. You and all your evil little minions, too!"

Kavik walked up behind the woman he had been guarding for more than 66 years. When she dropped to her knees to pray, he dropped down right beside her, offering his own prayers for the upcoming trip.

Chapter 6

Shana paced the motel room as she watched over a sleeping Nate and Charlie. Gideon and Mac had left hours ago, to meet with some local angels. But daylight would soon break on the horizon and the couple would be up and leaving for the hospital. She had no problem guarding both Nate and Charlie, but if something happened and they split up, she would have no choice but to stay with Nate. The thought of leaving Charlie unprotected had her chewing her lower lip with worry. Walking to the door, she stepped through it to look in the hallway to see if they were there. A nasty sensation sliding down her spine had her spinning back around.

"Well...well...well... all alone, are we?" The demon that stood in the middle of the room looked eerily human. Dressed in a gray suit with dark blonde hair slicked back from his forehead, he could easily pass for human if you looked past his solid black eyes, mouth full of razor-sharp teeth and the air of pure evil that surrounded him like cheap cologne.

Shana shifted her weight forward in case he rushed her, while letting her right hand drop casually near her sword.

"You must be Karau," she said calmly.

The demon before her inclined his head slightly in an old-fashioned manner. "I see my reputation precedes me. I'm assuming Gideon has told you about me, but I do wonder if he told you everything."

Shana didn't reply, allowing him to think whatever he wanted.

Karau casually walked around the room, running his fingertips across the desktop; then he picked up a bottle of Charlie's perfume. Bringing it to his nose, he inhaled deeply before smiling. "Ahhh... such a sweet and innocent fragrance... Sunflowers by Elizabeth Arden," he read on the bottle. "It suits her, I think." Casting a glance toward the sleeping woman, he arched a brow as he turned back to face Shana. "It would appear as if she is being neglected... surely the Mighty Gideon wouldn't abandon his post."

Again, Shana refused to answer, making Karau purse his lips at her in a mock frown.

"So, where *is* the girl's guardian? I don't see him anywhere..." He flashed himself over to stand near Charlie's side of the bed. He reached a hand out to stroke her cheek, only to grunt in pain a fraction of a second later when it was nailed to the wall by Shana's dagger. In another fraction of a second, he felt the searing pain of her sword thrust deeply into his chest as she stood between Karau and his intended target. The angel's crystal-blue eyes blazed with a holy vengeance as she stared him down.

"Make no mistake, hell rat -- I can protect them both from the likes of you!"

Shana's eyes grew wide when the demon's lips lifted in a mocking smile as he pushed himself forward on her sword until his abdomen rested against the hilt. Ignoring the green fluid that poured from the wound, he stared down at her.

"*You* make no mistake; you have no idea what *I'm* like." Then in a flash he disappeared, leaving a very shaken Shana holding tightly onto her now empty, and apparently useless, sword.

Gideon and Mac flew across the night sky until Mac pointed to a small alcove just ahead. Angling downward, they landed then quickly walked across the empty lot.

"I don't see the others but they should be here soon," Mac commented as he leaned against the brick wall to wait.

Gideon wasn't so comfortable. Keeping his hand near his sword, he carefully watched the skies. After fifteen minutes, had passed, Mac started to look worried.

"They should have been here by now. Something's not right."

"I agree. I think we need to head back to the hotel." A feeling of unease made his wings twitchy. Shifting his shoulders, he carefully searched the area, looking deeply into the shadows of the buildings.

"Why don't you head back? I will stay and wait and see if they show up," Mac offered.

Gideon immediately shook his head. "No, I don't want to split up. You are a sitting duck out here alone."

Mac frowned at the idea that Gideon didn't trust him to take care of himself. But before he could voice his complaint, Gideon held up his hand.

"It's not personal, Mac. I do not doubt your skills. I would say the same thing no matter who was here. With things happening like they are, it's just a bad idea to split up."

"Oh… okay then, but just so you know, I can take care of myself," Mac pointed out.

Gideon arched a brow at his comment. "Yeah, so can I, but I still found myself swinging over a really big pot of boiling demon soup. Like I said, it's not personal."

"Point taken," Mac said as he paled slightly at the description; then he lifted his hand. "Look, here they come!"

Just in the distance a group of at least twenty or more SA angels headed their way.

"I knew they would show!" Mac said with a grin.

After they had landed, two angels separated themselves from the others and walked quickly to where Gideon and Mac stood waiting. Bringing their arms across their chests, they inclined their heads in greeting.

"I am Rh'yan and this is Kalland. We have gathered who was available tonight. More will be coming to join us later."

"We are honored to be assisting you, Gideon. Your reputation is well-known. Tell us how we can be of help," Kalland said with another slight bow of respect.

"Thank you for coming. Has Mac informed you what we are dealing with?" Gideon asked.

"Not entirely, sir. Just that you needed our help." Rh'yan motioned for the other angels to step closer.

As briefly as possible, Mac and Gideon filled in the angels on what was taking place at the hospital and who was behind it. When he mentioned Karau's name, Rh'yan growled low in his throat.

"He is worse than any of them! Do you know why he looks so human? He is splicing human DNA into his own body. He is looking more and more human with every passing day. He needs to be destroyed!" Murmurs of agreement could be heard among the other SA angels.

"What's the point of becoming human?" Mac asked.

Kalland shook his head. "That I can't tell you, but he has a purpose, and it isn't anything good!"

"Maybe it's not becoming more human that's his goal but becoming less of a demon," Gideon suggested.

A little while later Gideon and Mac stepped into Charlie and Nate's hotel room only to quickly leap to the side to avoid being cut in half by Shana's sword.

"Whoa! Whoa! Whoa! It's only us!" he said to the guardian who was bearing down on him like a freight train.

Shana skidded to a stop when she saw Gideon's hands lifted in surrender. Letting her sword drop to her side, she collapsed in a nearby chair.

"Thank the Creator you're back!"

Looking quickly around the room, he saw nothing amiss. Both Charlie and Nate were still sleeping soundly. But Shana had a look on her face he had never seen there before… she looked *spooked.*

"What happened? Are you all right?" He took her sword, noting the green stain that covered it from tip to hilt.

"No…I'm not all right…I'm not even close to being all right. I just saw something that should have been impossible. I saw a demon that I had stabbed through with my sword act like nothing had happened. How is that possible?"

Gideon and Mac exchanged glances. "Start at the beginning and tell us everything."

After Shana had told everything, Gideon stood to his feet and walked over to the bed. "I can't risk leaving her again, not even with you. No offense."

Shana lifted her hand. "Hey, none taken. This guy has a creepy factor that's off the charts. Who is he and what exactly is his deal with you? And what is up with him looking so human? Seriously, if he wore sunglasses and kept his mouth shut he would totally pass for your average business man."

"Well, according to our new friends that we met tonight, Karau has been playing Mad Scientist with human DNA. Apparently, he has somehow been splicing it with his own," Mac said as he sat down. "We aren't sure why."

Shana stood to her feet and paced the room. "I bet that's why my sword didn't destroy him like it normally would. Our swords are designed to destroy *demons*. If he has enough human DNA to look basically human, then he may have enough to fool our weapons."

The implication of Shana's words settled on them like a dark cloud. If their weapons were useless against the enemy, then what?

"I know that someone is helping him do this, but who and why?" Gideon asked. Unfortunately, no one had any answers...

Faith's Legacy

Savanna Becker closely studied the strand of DNA under her microscope. The sample was destroying itself...again. Sighing, she rubbed her eyes and looked down at her notes, trying to spot what she was missing. Genetic modification was her specialty, so this shouldn't be any more difficult than splicing rat DNA, but it was proving to be substantially harder. Splicing the DNA together was easy enough. What she couldn't figure out was why the sample kept destroying itself. Looking back into the microscope, she watched as the cells multiplied; then before it could fully form, it would consume itself as if it was hungry. She paused as a crazy thought crossed her mind. She reached for a nearby scalpel and sliced it across her finger then let a drop of her blood fall into the petri dish. The mass of cells boiled and rolled until she thought it was going to come out of the dish, but then it settled back down. Peering back into the microscope, she saw the cells line up, divide and start to grow.

"Well, look at that. It requires blood. Of course, life requires blood!" she shouted in the empty lab. Knowing that she was close to solving the problem, she smiled. Karau was going to be *very* happy with her. Closing her eyes, she summoned the one whom she served.

Karau shimmered into view in Savanna's lab. The woman was a brilliant bio-engineer who specialized in genetic modification; she was also a follower of the dark arts, which made her very useful to him at the moment. Seeing her proud smile, he walked closer to see what she was holding out to him. Looking down into a small dish, he saw a small lump of gray that was wiggling slightly.

"I did it; I figured out why the spliced cells die. They need blood to grow. That's why you keep needing more injections."

Karau nodded as he studied the mass. Bringing his finger to his mouth, he bit down, letting a drop of green fluid drip down his finger into the dish. The mass writhed and rolled on the dish until it dissolved.

Savanna looked up at him crossly. "Well, I don't know what runs through your veins, but it's not the source of life."

"No, it's not. However, it does run through yours."

No one heard Savanna's screams as Karau took from her what he needed to accomplish his plan.

Wiping his mouth, Karau walked over to a nearby window and inspected his image. His eyes were still black, but after opening his mouth he saw that it was pink inside and filled with small square human teeth. He reached into the breast pocket of his suit and slipped on a pair of dark sunglasses. After he practiced smiling for a moment, he gave a self-satisfied nod.

"Close enough."

Stepping over Savanna's prone body, he opened the door and walked out...

Charlie bounced in place as she waited for her parents to get off the plane. She was so happy they were finally there!

"You look like a cocker spaniel puppy," Nate teased.

Charlie looked at him with a puzzled expression. "Why a cocker spaniel?"

Nate pointed at her hair which she had gathered into two low ponytails on each side of her head.

Charlie laughed. "Hey, it was quick and easy -- don't be hating on my tails."

"I like your tails; they are quite handy." He grabbed each ponytail gently and tugged Charlie to him, giving her a toe-curling kiss.

"Nathanial Jackson!" she scolded as she slapped at his shoulders, her cheeks now bright red.

"Hey, hey...here they come. Behave yourself," Nate said with a cheeky grin as he stepped back from her.

"Me behave?" was all Charlie had time to say before she was engulfed in Devon's embrace.

"Oh! Charlie-girl! It's so good to see you!" Pulling back, he studied her face, "Why is your face so red?"

Feeling her face turn even redder, Charlie just shook her head as she gave Nate the stink eye.

"Me next! Me next!" Sabrina cried as she reached for her daughter, pulling her into her arms. "Oh, you feel so good! I have missed you so much!"

Charlie felt tears well up in her eyes as she hugged her mother tightly. As much as she loved Nate and loved being his wife, she had not anticipated missing her mother like she had. "I missed you, too, Mama! So much!" She looked around for her brothers.

"Did the boys not come?"

"No, sweetie, they have school, so they are staying home with Seth," Sabrina explained.

Charlie slapped her palm to her forehead. "Of course! I wasn't even thinking about school. So, how is everyone at home? How is Stormy? I bet he is thinking I left him forever, huh?" she asked as they made their way back to the car.

"Everyone is doing fine, and yes, your horse always misses you when you're gone. I try to show him a little more attention, but he wants you," Devon replied.

"Cleo said to tell you that she will be here as soon as she can."

Charlie's face lit up when she heard her mother's words. "Cleo is really coming? Oh, my gosh! I'm so excited to see her! I miss her a lot."

"We all do. She has become family to us, but we must remember she has her own family who need her as much as we do," Sabrina pointed out.

"True," Charlie laughed.

After Sabrina and Devon had hugged and greeted Nate, they all got in the car to head back to the hotel where Charlie and Nate were staying.

"So. Fill us in on what's happened since we last spoke."

Nate wished he could tell Devon everything he knew about the situation, but there were a few things he had to keep to himself.

Charlotte squealed when she saw Gideon. Throwing her arms around his neck, she hugged him tightly, only letting go when Mac cleared his throat and pointed to himself.

"Can I get one of those?" he asked with a grin.

"Of course! I have missed you, too! It's so wonderful to see you both! Did you know that Cleo is coming and Kavik? It will be like old times!" she gushed with a bright smile.

Gideon smiled at Charlotte's enthusiasm as she hugged Mac and then Shana.

"She has been at def-con ten ever since she found out we were coming out here," Zareck said with a shake of his head, as he slapped Gideon's back in greeting.

Watching her excitedly tell Mac and Shana about their trip, Gideon felt his smile grow bigger. Charlotte did nothing by half-measures. He had grown close to his warriors when he was their leader, and with all the guardians of Charlie's family, but he would be telling an untruth if he said that the perky little angel with bare feet didn't hold a very special place in his heart.

An hour later everyone had settled into the rooms and was eating dinner. While their humans caught up on everything and enjoyed their meal, their angels enjoyed being together once more. Mac and Gideon told Zareck and Charlotte about Karau's newest plan.

"Well, that explains why he looked so human," Zareck commented. "I wondered about that the last time I saw him." He looked at Shana. "You say that he appears even more human now?"

"Yes, he does; his eyes and the inside of his mouth are still black, and he still has his demon teeth, but other than that he could easily pass as a human male. Did they tell you that my weapons had no effect on him? I got him with both my dagger and my sword and he just smiled at me. It was the creepiest thing I've even seen," she said with a shudder.

"Your weapons had no effect? None?" Charlotte asked with a look of dismay.

Shana shook her head back and forth, "No, ma'am. He didn't act like it bothered him in the least. In fact, he was amused by it."

"Well, that's not good. What on earth do we do if we can't use our weapons?" Charlotte asked with a look of uncertainty.

The angels looked at one another, all knowing that the game had just taken a serious turn.

Savanna smoothed the ace bandage around the wound in her arm where Karau had viciously bitten her three nights ago, in her lab. Luckily it didn't appear to be getting infected, which was a complete wonder. No telling where his disgusting teeth had been prior to sinking into her flesh. She hadn't seen the evil warlord since, but she was going to tell him off the next time she did. There was no need in his attacking her like that. She would have freely given him what he needed. He did it for pure sport and she wasn't going to stand for it! After pulling on her shirt, she pulled the sleeve down to cover the bandage. It would be well-hidden under her lab coat once she got to work, but she didn't want to answer any questions until then. Picking up her briefcase, she started for the door only to be stopped short when Karau shimmered into place right in front of her.

"Savanna, how nice to see you once more," he said in a silky-smooth voice. When he smiled, she was momentarily dazzled. It appeared her blood had helped him to transition even more. The smile he gave her would give Brad Pitt's a run for his money. But it would take more than a pretty set of pearly whites to make her forget what he did to her. Crossing her arms, she glared at him without responding.

"Oh, come now, my pet. Don't be angry with me," he crooned sweetly.

Emerald green eyes flashed sparks as she stared him down. "First off, I am *not, have never been and never will be,* your pet; we are *business* partners, and secondly, I am way beyond angry!"

To her surprise, he seemed somewhat ashamed as he lowered his head.

"I know. I behaved beastly. My apologies."

Savanna narrowed her eyes at him. He looked apologetic, but she knew better. A demon was incapable of feeling remorse. Even one that looked as handsome as Karau currently did.

"What do you want? I'm late for work," she snapped.

Stepping close, he lifted his hand to play with a brilliant red curl only to have it slapped away.

"Do not *ever* touch me again without my permission. Have I made myself clear? I will stop everything. I will not help you in any way if you so much as look at me wrong. Remember, you can't make me do anything I don't want to do."

Karau stood for moment before smiling at her once more, but it was the soft chuckle that sent chills down her spine.

"Ah, dear sweet Savanna. Need I remind you that I can make your life and the lives of your loved ones very, shall we say, *uncomfortable?*"

Rage tore through Savanna at his threat. Tossing her briefcase aside, she marched up to him and shoved hard against his chest, knocking him back a step.

"You *dare* to threaten my family? I created you! I can destroy you -- don't *you* forget that!"

The words were barely out of her mouth before she found herself flung across the room and slammed against the wall, knocking the breath out of her. Wheezing for air, she opened her eyes, but large black spots clouded her vision. As she slid to the floor in a heap, Karau knelt in front of her, sliding the dark glasses to the top of his head. She stared into his soul-less black eyes as he smiled at her.

"Puny little human, you have no idea with whom you are dealing. I am not some human male that you can push around with your little potions and curses. I created you; every dark gift you have comes from me. Do you think I cannot take them away just as easily? You have no power in this relationship except what I allow you to have. Do not push me, for you will find that I can push back much harder." He stood and offered her his hand to help her up.

    Ignoring his gesture, Savanna stood to her feet on her own. Swaying slightly, she leaned against the wall. Karau had just scared her enough to remind her of exactly what she had forgotten…that he was a demon from the pits of hell. She had gotten too comfortable with him and his human exterior. She decided right then and there somehow, some way she was going to send him straight back to where he belonged.

Chapter 7

Charlie grinned after she hung up the phone then turned to look at her parents.

"I can't wait for you to meet Brody and Pastor Tony!"

"Brody is definitely a character," Nate agreed with a smile.

A few minutes later there was a light tap on the door. Nate opened it and then made the introductions.

Brody smiled his megawatt smile. "Most pleased to meet you. Your offspring is totally charming." Lifting Sabrina's hand, he placed a kiss across her knuckles. "I see where she gets it."

Sabrina blushed as Charlie cracked up, "Is she a rad A-frame, too?"

Brody nodded as he winked at Sabrina, "Totally an A-frame."

When Sabrina lifted confused eyes to Brody, Nate chuckled. "Don't worry, I'm not exactly sure what an A-frame is, but I think it's a good thing!"

Pastor Tony playfully nudged Brody out of the way. "Pay no attention to this surfer, Mrs. Lane. He is harmless. It really is a pleasure to meet you. I've become quite fond of your daughter and her husband in the short time I have known them."

Devon shook hands with Brody and Pastor Tony before pulling Sabrina safely back under his arm. Brody was just a shade too charming for his liking. In his mind, the only one allowed to kiss her sweet knuckles was him!

Sabrina smiled up at her husband. Even after almost fifteen years of marriage he occasionally let the green-eyed monster get the best of him. But she didn't mind. A *little* jealousy occasionally makes a woman feel appreciated and wanted. But he needn't worry. Devon was still an extremely handsome man, even if his blonde hair was now shot through with a little gray and his eyes were bracketed with laugh lines. He still made her heart skip a beat and she had eyes for no other.

After everyone had been seated, Pastor Tony spoke. "So, I'm assuming that you have been caught up on what's been taking place?"

Devon nodded. "Yes, and I'm sorry to say that will not be my first rodeo with this type of situation. I ran security in a bar years ago, that had a similar problem. I actually caught a demon on video. It was an eye-opening experience, and it scared me enough that I turned to Christ. I decided that if there were two teams, I certainly didn't want to be on theirs."

"Unfortunately, that's the reason that a lot of people turn to our Lord, but I figure he doesn't mind. If scaring the devil right out of us is what it takes, then so be it," Pastor Tony replied.

Devon chuckled. "I admit I'm not scared of much. I can hold my own against most things, but when I saw that thing crawling across the ceiling of that bar, I knew I had just encountered something that I had no defense against, at least not at the time."

"But you do feel differently now, yes?" Pastor Tony asked with a serious expression.

"You bet I do. I know now that greater is he that is in me than he who is in the world. I don't play with them."

"And do you feel the same?" he asked of Sabrina.

"Yes, sir. Although I haven't had the experience that my husband has, I know that God gave us authority over evil."

"Good...good. I need to know that you know your strength and your power, because the very first thing the enemy will try to do is tell you that you have none. Right now, we know what the devil is doing, but we don't know why. Not that the why really matters because we will stop him."

"What should we do first?" Nate asked.

"I want us to go to the hospital because for now that is ground zero, our place of battle. I believe you said that you have more people coming?"

"Yes, my family is coming. They should all be here within a couple of days. They are all very strong Christians as well," Sabrina answered.

"Excellent. I will have members of my church also join us; however, we must do this cautiously, only taking a few members inside at a time. We don't want the other visitors or patients becoming alarmed at what we are doing, for most won't understand it. I understand that Dr. Reed has given us permission, but let's not disrupt the hospital's day-to-day routine. I feel as large as the hospital is, we can send in fifteen to twenty warriors at a time. We will go in pairs of two and three, because of joint anointing. Matthew 18:20 states where two or three are gathered in his name he is with them. I want every possible advantage that we can get."

Pastor Tony then anointed each one there. They joined hands and formed a circle as he prayed for power and protection. After he was done, Brody clapped his hands.

"Whew! I can feel it! The Lord is with us! Let's go kick some serious demon booty!" They all laughed and agreed that they felt the presence of God as well as they all walked out.

As the angels flew next to the cars that carried their humans, Zareck looked over at Gideon. "You know the surfer was right. I can feel God's power with us. Do you feel it?"

Gideon nodded. "Most definitely. Pastor Tony is a force to be reckoned with, and the rest are no slouches either."

Jerking his head back toward the dark blue sedan that carried Brody and Pastor Tony, Zareck asked what they knew about their guardians.

"Not a thing, actually. Let's get Mac to go visit with them. I'm still not used to having an SA angel handy to do things like this." Gideon dropped back to fly next to Mac.

"Have you spoken to Brody and Pastor Tony's guardians?"

Throwing him an insulted look, Mac answered, "Of course, I have! It would be rather rude not to speak to them, don't you think?"

Gideon smiled. "My apologies. I was just telling Zareck that I'm still unaccustomed to you and your ability to see all of us. What are their names?"

"Brody has a female named Sabra, and Pastor Tony's is a male named Maxon, who, by the way, is at least part warrior angel. His wings are a dark gray and his amour is a lot like yours."

Gideon nodded. "I am not surprised to hear that. He is a strong man spiritually. I would imagine that his light attracts a lot of attention from the enemy."

Faith's Legacy

"Most assuredly, and it's only going to get worse before this is over with," Mac replied with a grim look.

Savanna sat in the middle of the pentagram that she had drawn on the floor in the center of her candle-lit living room. In front of her was a bowl filled with herbs and other various ingredients. Closing her eyes, she chanted the spell to prevent Karau from coming near her or her family. Swaying back and forth slightly, she let the words spill from her lips faster and faster as she felt the steady increase of energy in the room. The air crackled and wind began to whip through the apartment. When the moment was right, she opened her hand and sliced across her palm, letting her blood drip into the bowl. Flames flared up in the bowl briefly before dying back down to a glowing ember. The room was now calm and silent as the smoke drifted across it. Opening her eyes, Savanna smiled. She wasn't the head priestess of this region for nothing. Karau might be all-powerful, but she wasn't without skills. Getting up, she cleared away the bowl and swept away the chalk pentagram. Turning on her lights, she gasped in horror when she saw not only Karau standing where she had just performed a banishment spell but six other demons as well.

Karau slowly clapped his hands as he approached. "That was a wonderful show, Savanna. Now tell me just who were you trying to banish? Hmmm? Was it someone I know, perhaps?" Glancing back, he smiled at the other demons who were with him. "Do you think it was *me* she was trying to banish?" The demons all laughed, if the hacking wheezing noises they made could be called laughter. Turning back to Savanna, he gave her a look of sad disappointment as he sighed dramatically. "You know, you're really are starting to hurt my feelings. Why, if I didn't know better, I would say that you didn't want to be friends anymore."

"I don't want to be your friend anymore! I don't want anything more to do with you! Now get out of my apartment and stay away from me and my family!" Savanna screamed out.

Faith's Legacy

"But, my dear, if we aren't friends, then that means we must be enemies. Do you know how I treat my enemies? Surely you do, or need I remind you?" Lifting his hand, he circled his arm around his head, which was the signal for the others to rip around the apartment destroying everything they could get their claws on. Within seconds everything she owned was in tatters.

Savanna stood with clenched fists, tears streaming down her face, shaking her head in defiance. "It doesn't matter. I'm done with you! I won't help you anymore!"

Karau studied her for a moment before flashing himself right in front of her. **"You will be done when I say you're done!"** he screamed in her face right before he launched his vicious attack.

Savanna's last thought before she blacked out was she had made a horrible mistake and she prayed that it wasn't too late to fix it.

Charlie sat in the waiting room with her Bible open across her lap. She had been there since early that morning and it was now approaching six in the evening. Ever since she woke up, she had a craving for God's Word and had kept her nose in it all day, stopping only to speak to people who came in and out of the waiting area or to pray when she felt directed to do so. Pastor Tony's words about her being a strong leader still had her worried that she simply didn't know enough. Closing her eyes, she once more prayed that God would give what she needed to see this through.

"That's a lovely book of fairy tales that you're reading. Tell me, do you have a favorite story?"

Opening her eyes, she saw an attractive woman with flaming red hair studying her. The woman looked like she had been in a car accident. The entire right side of her face was bruised a deep shade of purple. Bloodshot green eyes watched her carefully. Looking closer, Charlie changed her mind. The woman had not been in an accident -- she had been beaten and very badly. She could clearly see that the dark bruises around her throat were in the shape of a man's fingers.

"I'm sorry. What did you say?" Charlie asked. Even though she clearly heard the woman's words, she couldn't believe she had said them.

The woman pointed her finger at the book open in Charlie's lap. "Your book, it's full of very interesting stories. I was asking which was your favorite." Her voice sounded rough and broken.

Before Charlie could respond, she felt goosebumps race across her skin as the Holy Spirit spoke to her. *"Be very careful, this woman is possessed by evil."*

"This book has so many wonderful stories that I'm not sure I could pick a favorite." She paused as the woman seemed to be looking at something just to the left of her. Casually shifting in her seat, Charlie glanced in the direction that the woman was staring but saw nothing. "Have you read it?" she asked.

The woman's eyes jerked back to Charlie almost as if she had forgotten she was there. "What? Oh, yes, well… I've heard of the stories in it. It all seems rather farfetched to me."

Charlie smiled as she furiously prayed silently. "How so? Do you not believe in God?"

The woman seemed to be growing more and more uncomfortable by the second, shifting her eyes all around the room, looking everywhere except directly at Charlie. In a rush of love and compassion that she couldn't understand, Charlie set the Bible next to her on the seat and leaned forward.

"God loves you. He wants you to know that no matter what you have done it's not too late. He loves you so very much!"

The woman's eyes grew wide with shock and surprise, before an ugly sneer twisted her mouth. "There is no God. Only fools believe in such garbage," she spat out.

"Then I guess I'm a fool because I believe with every fiber of my being. You know what? I'm going to pray for you. I don't know your name or your story but Jesus does…"

At the mention of the name of Jesus, the woman bolted out of her seat and ran from the waiting room. Charlie jumped up to go after her when that same voice spoke to her again.

"It's okay, let her go. You planted the seed. Now it will grow."

Faith's Legacy

Gideon had stood while the woman spoke with Charlie. He wasn't sure if she could see him or only felt his presence, but she kept staring right where he was standing. The poor thing was being controlled by an evil spirit. But it seemed to be struggling to maintain its grip on her. The woman did not seem to be a willing host.

Nate and Brody came to the waiting room a few minutes after the woman had left. Charlie was still in shock about what happened.

"Honey, it was the strangest thing! It's like I could feel her desperation. She wants to reach out to God but she is scared and something seems to be stopping her. I have never seen this woman before in my life but I felt such an overwhelming love for her!"

Brody smiled as he placed his hand on her shoulder. "You felt the love that God has for this woman and for all of us. At least to the extent that you could handle it."

Charlie smiled as she laughed softly while placing her hand over her heart.

"That was intense! I hope I didn't freak her out too badly."

That made Brody snort in laughter. "If meeting the great Kahuna doesn't freak you out, then you didn't do it right!"

Nate pulled Charlie into his arms. "I'm really proud of you, babe. God spoke and you listened. I have a feeling we will be seeing our mystery woman again."

Hearing her sniffle against his shirt, he pulled her back and studied her face.

"Why the tears?" he asked.

"Oh, Nate! She was just so lost! Her heart and soul are craving light and love but she is lost in the darkness screaming for help, but no one can help her."

"But someone did -- you did. She knows who to find to help her," Nate said as he brushed the tears from her face.

"I hope she will… I really hope that she will."

"Let's pray for her right now," Brody suggested. They held hands and lifted the unknown woman to the throne of heaven.

Faith's Legacy

Savanna ran from the hospital as if the hounds of hell were chasing her. Actually, the hounds of hell she could handle; it was the look of pure love burning in that young woman's eyes she had to get away from. Never had she seen such an intense look that wasn't filled with hate and malice. She had no idea that love could be used like a weapon. But the blonde girl had wielded it well. She would make sure to avoid her in the future. Once she was off the hospital grounds, she felt confused instead of better because now she had the overwhelming urge to turn around and go back!

"No way... Karau can find someone else to deal with her," she muttered under her breath. After he had beaten her up spiritually and physically the night before, she knew she had to find a way to escape his clutches. Even after casting the most powerful spell she knew, he was still able to do what he wanted to her. Hopelessness filled her heart at the thought of forever being the demon's slave.

"Savanna."

Spinning around, Savanna looked with frightened eyes for whoever was calling her name. Searching the street, she saw no one that seemed to be paying any attention to her.

"Savanna, I love you."

There it was again. That soft voice. It was warm and soothing, and it called to her, making her slow her steps as if she were about to turn around. Shaking her head, she cried out.

"Leave me alone!" as she took off running again when everything in her wanted to turn around and seek out the source of love.

Once more Charlie was dancing with excitement at the airport. Today was the day that Cleo was coming and she couldn't wait to see the woman who had been like a second mother to her. Devon was the one to spot her first since his height gave him a better vantage point.

"There she is!" he said.

Charlie strained to see her. Finally, after a few moments she saw a colorful head wrap and knew it had to be her Cleo. Unable to wait for her, she walked as quickly as she could in her direction, finally breaking into a run when their eyes met.

Dropping her bags at her feet, Cleo stood with her arms outstretched and waited for Charlie to run into them.

"Oh, *merci*, child. I have missed you so!" Cleo whispered as she held Charlie and swayed from side to side, uncaring of the curious eyes that she felt upon them. *Let them look,* she thought. *Let them see that love does not see color!*

"I almost couldn't believe it when Mama said you were coming!"

Cleo held her shoulders firmly and gave her a stern look. "When have you ever known me not to come when you needed me? You know I feel as if you're my own child."

"You have always been there for me; I'm sorry. I didn't mean it the way it sounded," Charlie explained.

"It's all right, baby girl, no harm done. Now tell me -- are you happy with your young man?"

The smile that Charlie gave her was answer enough. "Oh, yes! I love him so much and he is so sweet to me, Cleo! It's really like a fairy tale, well, maybe a slightly twisted fairy tale with all this other that's taking place."

When the others had finally made their way to where Cleo and Charlie were standing, Sabrina quickly stepped in for a tight hug from her dearest friend.

Sabrina felt tears prickle in her eyes as she inhaled the familiar scent of Cleo's perfume. It was rich, earthy, spicy and suited the woman perfectly.

Cupping Sabrina's face, Cleo shook her head. "I think I misspoke. Charlie must be like my granddaughter, for you are like my daughter! My daughter who I have missed something terrible!"

Sabrina laughed as she swiped quickly at her tears. "We have all missed you, too! It's so wonderful to see you. Really, it shouldn't take something like this to get us together. We all need to be spanked!"

Devon reached down and grabbed the bags after he had grabbed a hug first. Nate stood back, just a little uncertain about how he should approach this woman that he had known for most of his life but hadn't yet established a relationship. Cleo saw him and took care of all uncertainty when she reached over and yanked him to her.

"I be not knowing why you're standing off over there like a stranger, Nate Jackson! You best get over quick fast and give old Cleo a hug!"

Nate laughed as he was engulfed in a tight hug and returned the hug just as tightly.

"All right, now that we have shown everyone in this airport what love looks like, I think we best be heading to the hotel. I suspect that you have a lot to tell me that doesn't need to be told in mixed company."

Kavik grinned widely at the look of shock he was getting from the other angels. Spinning slowly in a circle, he opened his wings and fanned them out so they could see every beautiful feather.

"Oh, my *goodness*, Kavik! Your wings are gorgeous! When did they grow back? Have they always been gray? Are you thrilled? You're thrilled, aren't you?" Charlotte fired off her questions in rapid succession as she sank her fingers into his soft gray feathers.

Kavik chuckled. "Slow down, little sister. One question at a time. They grew back nearly three weeks ago. I can't tell you how happy and surprised I was when it happened. I thought surely the Creator would make me wait until I returned to the heavens to restore them to me, if he decided to at all." When Charlotte opened her mouth, he lifted his hand and cupped her chin softly with his strong fingers, "And no, they were not always gray," he answered before she could repeat her question.

"Why, of course, he restored your wings! He loves you! Oh! I'm so happy for you I think I'm going to cry," Charlotte said as she sniffled happily.

Zareck rolled his eyes. "Creator, deliver us from weepy females," he teased, as he offered his hand to Kavik. "The wings look great, brother."

"Just out of curiosity, what color were they before?" Gideon asked as he admired Kavik's new wings.

They were white with gray patches, why?"

"Hmm... I've just noticed that when wings change color, that usually means something's about to change in their human's life, but that doesn't mean that's the case with you; maybe he just thought you could use a make-over."

The angels all stared in surprise then snorted at Gideon's unintended joke. Mac clapped a hand on his shoulder. "Good one, but don't quit your day job!"

Gideon felt the tips of his ears turn red at the other angel's gentle teasing.

On the way back, Gideon filled Kavik in on what all had happened. The tattooed angel scowled fiercely when he heard about Karau's latest obsession.

"He cannot become human any more than we can! It's impossible!" he protested.

"You saw him, Kavik, when he attacked us a couple of years ago. He looked human even then, and they say he looks even more so now. It is possible," Charlotte pointed out. "I don't understand it, but he is doing it."

"He has someone helping him. Karau might be smart, but he isn't this smart. He has a human accomplice somewhere. If we can find them, then maybe we can stop him from advancing any further, or, God forbid, create anymore. The last thing we need is a human/demon hybrid army to emerge," Zareck said.

Gideon nodded in agreement. "I had actually already considered that. Zareck, what do you think of assigning someone to him to follow him and find out who is helping him and where they are doing it?"

Zareck frowned, "One of us? Who will protect our humans?"

Mac stepped up from the back of the group. "I can assign an SA angel. I think that's what Gideon had in mind as well, unless I'm mistaken." He looked over at Gideon to confirm his guess and saw him nodding his head.

"That's exactly what I was thinking, Mac. You can choose who you feel would be best suited for this. Meanwhile we need to figure out how to secure the hospital from any more attacks. I would like to be able to keep out as many demons as we can." He lifted his hand when Zareck started to speak. "I'm aware that we cannot keep them all out. Those who are with a willing host we can't touch, but we can stop the ones who are entering on their own to cause trouble."

"Won't the family's prayers help, too?" Charlotte asked.

"More so than anything else, but we still need to do our part," Gideon replied, as he turned back to Mac.

"You go and get someone on Karau. The quicker we find out just who is helping him, the faster we can hopefully find a way to make them stop. Oh, and Mac, assign as many SA angels as you can find to guard the hospital at all times. Tell them to stop anything that isn't attached to a human."

After Mac flew off to do as Gideon instructed, the angels all went back to their humans.

Chapter 8

Karau paced Savanna's lab, growing more and more impatient with each passing second. He was losing control of her and he had to find a way to regain it if he ever hoped to raise his army of human/demon hybrids.

"Where is she?" he bellowed loudly, causing the four low-ranking demons to tremble in fear. "Go find her and bring her to me," he ordered. Just before the last demon could shimmer from view, he grabbed it up by its neck, bringing its face mere inches from his own.

"And do *not* fail." The promise of a swift and terrible punishment did not need to be spoken aloud. It was all there in his black eyes.

Savanna huddled in the back of the church trying not to be ill. She had always given this particular church a wide berth because she could feel the power that radiated from it. But she figured that if it made her this uncomfortable, then surely Karau or any of his flunkies would not be able to enter. She needed time to think, to decide what her options were, if she even had any. One thing she knew for sure was she was finished helping him. He would be furious when he discovered that she had tricked him. In the beginning, he was getting DNA from patients at the hospital, even going so far as to kill most that he took from. But what he didn't know was that she didn't use the DNA he collected. She used her own, for no other reason but insurance to make sure that he would always need her; therefore, it offered her some protection. But her plan backfired on her. She didn't think she would ever not want to participate in his plan. Karau had offered her everything she could ever want and had even started to deliver on a few of his promises, but it was costing Savanna her soul. She could feel it. With every procedure, she could feel his claws sinking deeper and deeper into her spirit, and now she wasn't sure if she could ever get him out.

That's why she was now huddled in the back of Hope for the Lost church. If anyone was lost, it was most certainly her. She just wasn't sure if she wanted to be found or not.

Pastor Tony unlocked the back door of the church and headed toward his office to work on next Sunday's sermon, but before he could reach it, he stopped. He had the feeling he wasn't alone. Placing his keys and Bible on a table in the hallway, he quietly walked toward the sanctuary, checking various rooms as he went. Finally, he stood at the front of the sanctuary.

"Hello? My name is Pastor Tony. I know someone is here. Why don't you show yourself so we can get better acquainted? If you're hungry, we have a kitchen in the back. I'd be happy to prepare you a warm meal." He waited and listened but heard nothing, so he slowly walked down the aisle, checking each pew. Finally, when he had reached the next to the last row, he saw her. A woman with beautiful red hair huddled on the floor between the pews. She looked at him with green eyes that were both frightened and wary. She was also badly beaten. Not wishing to cause her more fear, he took a seat in a pew across the aisle and gave her a warm and welcoming smile.

"Her name is Savanna," the Holy Spirit whispered.

"Hello, Savanna, I'm Pastor Tony. Why don't you let me help you?" he asked softly. The woman's eyes grew wide when he called her by name.

"How...how did you know my name?" she asked.

"Because God told me. He knows all of his children's names."

Savanna shook her head and tried to curl up into an even smaller ball. "I'm not his child. He hatessss me," she mumbled as a spasm racked her body.

Tony instantly went on alert. He saw the signs of possession that she was starting to display, the slurred speech, refusing to make eye contact and now the body tremors.

"That's not true, Savanna. God loves you very, very much. In fact, he loves you enough that he made sure that I was here today to help you. I'm normally not at the church on Tuesdays, but I felt like I needed to be here. I thought perhaps I needed extra time to prepare my sermon for Sunday, and now I know that I'm here to help you."

"Lies! It's all lies!" she spewed out in a voice that was much lower than it was just a second ago.

"Be quiet, demon! I am speaking to Savanna! I command you to be silent in the name of Jesus!" Tony ordered with a voice full of authority.

Savanna moaned and jerked as a line of spittle formed on her mouth.

"Savanna, the devil has been telling you lies. God does love you and it doesn't matter what you have done; it doesn't matter... do you hear me? The cross covered all sin, even the worst of the worst. God loves you and right now his arms are reaching out to you to pull you out of the darkness. Look at me, Savanna! Look up at me!" he commanded.

Savanna opened her eyes and tried to lift her head from the soft green carpet of the sanctuary to do as the pastor instructed, but it was so hard. Her head felt like it weighed a million pounds, as if something had it held in a vice grip.

"Devil! You let go of her right now!"

Savanna's head suddenly popped up like it was mounted on a spring. Looking upward she saw the pastor, surrounded by a beautiful white light. In his eyes, she saw the same all-consuming love that she had seen in the girl's eyes at the hospital. She didn't understand it, but she wanted it. If only she could have it. Her fingers twitched on the carpet, as her body tried to reach for the light.

"Savanna, reach out for me. Simply lift your hand and show me that you want my help. I will do the rest; just take one small step."

Savanna shook her head as despair filled her heart. "It's too late... he has my soul...Karau has it... I gave it to him." She gagged as her stomach heaved mightily, causing her to curl up once more face down on the carpet. She could feel a burning like acid on her legs and arms as unseen claws dug deep into her skin, dragging her down into a dark pit.

Tony dropped to his knees and fell flat on his stomach less than two feet from where Savanna lay weak and clearly under attack.

"He won't let me go," she sobbed weakly.

"He will if you want him to, but you have to tell me. I can't make it leave unless you say you want it gone." When Savanna made no reply, he pounded the floor with his fist to get her attention. When she opened her eyes again, he spoke. "I'm right here with you. Can you see me? Honey, reach out your hand to me -- I can pull you out. God loves you! God loves you! Let him save you! It's not too late! Reach. Out. Your. Hand!" Tony screamed the last part, fearing she was going to lie right there and die. But he saw the fingers of her left-hand twitch then start to slowly inch their way across the carpet in his direction. She lifted her head and whispered the words he had been waiting for.

"Make… him…leave…" Her words were barely audible but it was enough. Reaching in his pocket, he grabbed a small bottle of anointing oil. Twisting off the cap, he poured the oil into his hand then placed it on Savanna's head, causing her to twist and groan as she tried to crawl away from him. But Tony climbed on top of Savanna to keep her from crawling away.

"Devil, your time is up! I command you in the name of Jesus to come out of Savanna right now! She no longer welcomes you."

Savanna screeched and clawed desperately at the carpet, trying to get away. "It hurts! He is killing me!" she cried out.

"Devil, you release her now!" Tony once more demanded.

"Noooo… Leave me alone! She is miiiine!" This time the voice was low and demonic.

"Help me, preacher! They are dragging me to hell! Help meee!" Savanna wailed.

The terror in her voice told Tony that the enemy wasn't letting go without a fight. "No, they aren't. It's just a trick. God won't let them have you." Spotting a visitor Bible in the back of the pew, he grabbed it and placed it on Savanna's back.

"Devil, I command you to release her right now in the mighty name of JESUS!"   Reaching out, he grabbed both of her arms and pulled with all his might.

The four demons hanging onto Savanna screeched, as did the demon that was being expelled. Savanna was being pulled from their grasp. The man of God wouldn't let her go. Now with one mighty pull the power of God blasted her from their clutches, sending them tumbling across the church. The demons' last sight was the face of God's mighty angel descending with his fiery sword swinging towards them...

Tony lay on the carpet on his back with the woman sprawled halfway across him. Never in all his many years in the Lord's service had he needed to physically pull someone from Satan's grasp. But he did today. He gently pushed her from him and rolled her until she was face up on the carpet. She was moaning softly and panting as if she had just run the Boston Marathon.

"Savanna? Are you okay?" he asked as he gently stroked her face.

Opening her eyes, Savanna looked up into the most beautiful face she had ever seen. This man had saved her very soul from being pulled into hell!

"You saved me," she whispered, looking up at him in awe. "How can I ever thank you?"

Tony smiled down at her as he shook his head. "No, ma'am. God saved you. It was his power that drove back the darkness, not mine. Do you think you can sit up?" He carefully pulled her into a sitting position. The stark look in her eyes and the paleness of her face were a testament of what she had just gone through.

Lifting a shaky hand to her face, Savanna tried to process what just happened. Looking down at her arms and legs, she was surprised to find them unharmed, for she felt the claws digging in deep trying to hold her.

Tony saw her look at her arms and knew what she was looking for. "It was all an illusion, Savanna. The demons wanted you to think that they had you, but it was a lie. Once you decided to reach out to God, they no longer had any power over you," Tony explained.

"I'm sorry. I don't understand any of this." She paused then looked up at him. "I'm a witch. I... I...just felt like you should know what I am."

Tony was not totally surprised by her admission. He knew she had been playing with something truly dark for the devil to have such a grip on her.

"Do you intend to stay a practicing witch? If your answer is yes, then all that we have done today will be for naught. It doesn't matter what name you give it, black witch, white witch, sorceress, enchantress, Wicca, black magic, white magic, voodoo -- it's all part of the occult and it all belongs on Satan's playground."

Savanna looked confused as well as simply worn out. "I don't know what I'm going to do. I don't know anything else. But I know I don't want him to have control over me again. I don't want to help him anymore!" Tears fell like rain down her cheeks as she sobbed, hiding her face in her hands.

Tony felt his heart break for the poor woman who still looked so lost. "Tell you what, my dear. We don't have to make any decisions right this second. You look like you could use a good meal and a long nap." Getting to his feet, he helped Savanna to hers. "First, let me tell you that you are safe here. You have nothing to fear from me or anyone who is a member of this church. Now why don't you follow me to the kitchen? We will have a nice bowl of chicken enchilada soup with corn chips; doesn't that sound good?"

When he smiled down at her, Savanna couldn't help but return it. "Yes, that actually does sound really good."

She followed him into a brightly-lit kitchen where a small round table was covered with a red and green plaid tablecloth that reminded her of Christmas. Sitting down at the table, she ran her hand over the soft material and felt tears prickle at the back of her eyes once more. Not knowing what else to do, she let them gather and fall unchecked down her face. Somehow, they felt good, as if they were washing away her sins.

Tony quickly heated up the pot of soup that he had prepared the day before. Savanna had been sitting at the table staring down at the tablecloth, quietly weeping ever since she sat down.

"Oh, Heavenly Father, reveal to me what to say to your daughter who is so lost," he prayed silently.

Faith's Legacy

"Love her, and tell her that I love her," the Holy Spirit whispered.

Once the soup was nice and warm, he carried it and two glasses of tea to the table then took a seat across from Savanna. Reaching over, he took her hand then bowed his head.

"Precious Lord, I want to thank you for allowing me to be here today to help Savanna. Father, I pray that you will continue to show yourself to her in a mighty way. Open her eyes and ears to see and hear your truth. I pray a hedge of protection around her to protect her from the enemy. Bless this food, Lord. Amen."

When he lifted his head after praying, he found Savanna staring at him with an odd look.

"What is it?" he asked.

"You just spoke to him like he was right here," she said in amazement.

Tony chuckled as he sprinkled some chips into his soup. "Well, that's because he is right here. Where did you think he was?"

"I don't know. To be honest, I haven't given God much thought. He didn't seem very interested in me so I returned the favor."

"Why did you think he wasn't interested? He gave you life every morning, didn't he? That sounds like he was pretty interested to me." Tony gestured with his spoon for Savanna to eat. Dipping her spoon into her bowl, she took a small bite.

"Wow...this is great." She offered the compliment as she took another bite.

"Try it with the corn chips," Tony suggested as he pushed the bowl of chips toward her.

She smiled again after trying the chips in her soup. "You're right -- the chips make it even better."

They both finished their soup; then Tony got up to clear away the dishes. He shook his head when Savanna started to get up to help.

"No, you stay seated. This won't take but just a second. Why don't you tell me what made you decide to become a witch? It all seems a little scary to me."

Savanna made a scoffing noise before answering his question. "Yeah, it can be. I've only recently discovered that aspect of it. Up until then, I enjoyed it."

Tony was careful to keep his voice interested and not condemning. He wanted to keep her talking and he was truly curious what made her choose that lifestyle. "What was your favorite part, you know, of being a witch?"

Savanna paused as she thought over his question. Finally, she answered, "The feeling of power, of being able to control that which most people fear."

Tony turned around and leaned against the counter. "Then what happened that made you hide in my church? It looked like you were scared to death, and, not to be rude, but your face looks like someone kicked it."

Putting a hand to her face, Savanna got up and walked to the back door. She looked out through the multi-planed window as she wrapped her arms around her middle. "I was scared to death...I still am...he is out there...waiting." Her words were spoken so softly Tony almost couldn't make them out.

"Who is waiting for you, Savanna? Who are you so afraid of? Who did that to you?" He kept his voice low and soft to match hers.

Shaking her head, she swiped at the tears that had once more started to flow. "It doesn't matter. You can't stop him. I tried. If I can't keep him away, no one can."

"So, where is the power you thought you had?"

Savanna shrugged slightly. "I don't know; either it was an illusion, too, or it was only mine as long as he allowed it. Maybe it was both."

"In the end, what did being a witch, a follower of darkness, what did it leave you with?"

When she didn't answer, he reached out and turned her around to face him. "Savanna, all your power, all your gifts, where are they now?"

She stared up at him still shaking her head and weeping. "I don't know... I don't know anything anymore."

"But you did know where to come for help, didn't you? You came to my church. Why is that? There are churches all over -- why mine?"

Now starting to shake, Savanna pushed away from his grasp to walk across the room, putting some distance between them.

"Savanna?"

Spinning around, she glared at him, "The power! I could feel the power that came from this place! I hated it. It was like it mocked me every time I passed."

Tony took three steps forward, putting himself right in front of her. "That's real power, Savanna. The power of God makes a mockery of Satan and what power he claims to have. You see, he only has the power that you allow him to have over you. He is a grand manipulator and a liar. He is like a magician, all smoke and mirrors and sleight of hand. He has no real power; he just knows a few tricks. What you felt coming from this place is *true* power."

Rubbing her chest, Savanna drew in a deep breath. "I can feel that it's gone. Will it come back?"

Tony shrugged his shoulders. "If you don't fill that space with something else, then it could."

"You mean God, don't you?" she sighed. "I don't think he wants to live in there. I'm sure it's pretty messy."

"Well, you see, God is really good at cleaning up messes. In fact, he would like nothing better than for you to invite him in. He would have your little heart all clean and shiny in no time."

"Would he really want me? Even after what I was? I have done some terrible things. Things that would make your skin crawl, preacher man." As if the weight of every one of her sins now weighed on her shoulders, she pulled her chair back out and fell into it. Bracing her elbows on the table, she rubbed hard at her temples.

Tony sat back down as well. "Do you think that you are a surprise to God? He knew what you were going to do before you did. He knows every dark secret, every evil thought and act. He knows it now and he knew it two thousand years ago, when he was hanging on that cross, bloodied and beaten for you. He not only loves you -- He loves you enough to die for you, to take your punishment so you wouldn't have to. Savanna, the devil gives you gifts, but only with some very serious strings attached. I think you know that now. But God only wants to love you and give you good things. He wants a relationship with you. Do you realize that when you were in your mother's womb that God created a place in your heart that was just for him? People try to fill that spot with a lot of different things, sex, drugs, alcohol; and some try to fill it with a feeling of power. But only God goes there and only God can fill that space."

Savanna looked up at him sadly. "I'm not good enough. I can't be good enough to be what you are."

Tony smacked his hand down on the table, "That is the biggest lie that the devil uses! Honey, no one is good enough! Not me or anyone else. That's what the cross was for. Jesus died because he was good enough for *all* of us. It's by his blood that we are made worthy. When a person accepts Jesus as their Lord, something happens. The blood of Jesus covers that person, washing away all their sins and making them righteous before God. When God looks at a person who has been saved, do you know what he sees?"

"What?" Savanna asked.

"He sees us through the blood of his son, Jesus. He doesn't see our ugly sins, only Jesus. That's how we can be good enough, by accepting Jesus and his precious gift."

Tony could see hope start to shimmer in Savanna's beautiful green eyes. Reaching over, he took her hand in his.

"Savanna, remember when I said that all you had to do was reach out and I would save you? That's all you need to do right now. Just reach out to God and ask him to save you; ask him to wash your heart clean and make you acceptable to him. Do you want to do that?"

Unable to speak from the huge lump in her throat, Savanna could only nod.

"Then repeat these words after me." Bowing her head with Pastor Tony, she softly repeated the sinner's prayer...

Across town Karau felt the spiritual tether he had on Savanna snap when she said the sinner's prayer and invited Christ into her heart. His rage knew no bounds when he realized that his plans were ruined. It had him flipping tables and smashing the multimillion dollar instruments that had filled Savanna's lab.

"**Does she think she can simply walk away from me?**" he roared as he pulled over cabinets and flung glassware across the room, embedding it deeply into the walls. Finally, he stopped after everything had been demolished. Taking a deep breath, he ran his fingers through his hair, combing it back into place; then he straightened his tie and disappeared.

Chapter 9

The next morning Nate and Charlie were rattled out of their sleep by a loud pounding on their door.

"Who in the world would be here this early?" Charlie grumbled as she tried to bury her head under the pillow.

"I don't know. It's barely even daylight outside. Something must be wrong," Nate replied as he slipped on his prosthesis then stepped into his jeans.

The concern in Nate's voice had Charlie popping her head up from the covers and scrambling to grab her wrap. By the time Nate had thrown on a shirt and made it to the door, she was standing near the couch. Nate peeked through the peephole and saw Pastor Tony standing on the other side. Quickly unlocking the door, he let him in only to find that he wasn't alone.

Charlie stared in shock and surprise to see the woman that she had been praying for standing next to Pastor Tony.

"I don't believe it! It's you!" she said in astonishment.

Tony looked from Savanna to Charlie in confusion. "Do you two know one another?"

Charlie smiled as she shook her head. "Not exactly." Then she walked over to the woman. She held out her hand. "Hi, I'm Charlie Jackson and this is my husband, Nate, and you have no idea just how happy I am to see you!"

Savanna smiled shyly as she took Charlie's outstretched hand. "I'm Savanna Becker, and I don't know why anyone would be happy to see me right now."

Charlie looked up at Nate, who was looking just as confused as Pastor Tony. "Honey, this is the woman that I met in the waiting room, the one that we all prayed for."

Understanding lit up Nate's eyes as he smiled at Savanna. "Well, then I'm happy to see you, too, and in such good company."

Tony shook his head as he rubbed his face. "I guess I'm the only one still in the dark, but that's okay. You can fill me in later. Right now, I have something very important that we need to talk about."

Faith's Legacy

"Of course, why don't we all sit down? Honey, would you mind calling room service and have some coffee brought up?" Nate said as he studied Tony's tired eyes.

"Coffee sounds good, but while we are waiting on it, why don't you round up her folks? They need to hear this, too, and, quite frankly, I'm not up to repeating it twice."

Forty-five minutes later Charlie's family and Brody had joined them in their hotel room. They were all sipping on cups of steaming coffee, trying to get awake enough to listen to what Pastor Tony had to say.

"Let me first introduce you all to Savanna Becker, ex-witch and brand-new Christian." For the next few minutes he told them how he had met Savanna and what had happened in his church. "Now for the rest of what I want you to know, I will let Savanna tell you because it's really her story to tell."

Savanna stood nervously in front of the group of people who were all staring at her like she had grown another head until Charlie, the young woman she had met at the hospital, took pity on her.

"My goodness, she doesn't even know most of us, Pastor Tony. Why don't I make some introductions first?" Charlie quickly explained who everyone was.

"It's okay, Savanna. You can tell us whatever it was that you told Pastor Tony. We only want to help. Would you like some coffee?"

Savanna gave her a small smile as she waved her hand. "No, I'm nervous enough as it is. Coffee would only make it worse, thank you." Looking around the room, she shrugged her shoulders. "I don't know where else to start except at the beginning so that's where I'm starting. Like Tony said, I'm an ex-witch as of," she looked quickly down at the watch that was on her right wrist, "twelve hours ago, or so. Before I met Pastor Tony, I was actually helping..." she paused and looked over at Pastor Tony. "Are you positive they will believe me?" she asked.

"I promise you, my dear, these people understand the dark side. They will believe you," Tony assured her.

Faith's Legacy

Blowing out a deep breath, Savanna continued. "Okay, as I was saying. I was helping a demon named Karau. He has plans to recreate himself and build an army of hybrid demons to take over the world. I was helping by splicing human DNA into his. I was essentially making him human, or at least as close to human as possible." The room was in total silence after she had finished speaking. Everyone, including the angels, was staring at her in wide-eyed open-mouth shock.

"I know. It's a lot to take in, but I believe what she is saying is the truth," Pastor Tony said as he stood up next to her. "When she tried to tell it that she wasn't going to help him anymore, you can see what it did to her." He pointed to Savanna's bruised face. "I delivered this woman from one of the strongest possessions I have ever encountered. I literally had to pull her from its grasp. Whatever she was dealing with is very strong."

Devon held up his hand. "Please don't think we don't believe her; we just need a moment to take it all in. I have questions and I'm sure the others do, too."

"I will answer what questions I can," Savanna offered.

"How and when did you first encounter Karau?" Devon asked.

"As childish as this may sound, I summoned him up with a Ouija board about ten years ago," Savanna replied.

"You're kidding! Those things actually work?" Nate said.

Savanna nodded. "Oh, yes. I know they sell it as a children's toy, but it's a powerful tool and can open doors and let things in that you don't want in your homes. Take it from me -- stay as far away from them as you can."

"Can I ask *why* you would want to summon a demon?" This came from Sabrina.

Savanna shrugged once more. "To see if I could, honestly. I really didn't have any expectation that it would work."

"Were you a witch at the time?" Charlie asked.

"No, not really. I was curious about the dark arts. The movies and TV shows all made it look so exciting and fun, but after I was successful at summoning, I got in deeper and deeper."

"Where did you get the human DNA from?"

Savanna looked back at Devon.

"Karau would send his demons out to the hospital to collect DNA from the patients. But that's not the DNA I used." She paused and looked down at the ground. "I told him they didn't need to kill anyone to obtain DNA. He did it anyway. I'm...I'm so sorry for that."

Everyone exchanged guarded glances but no one commented on what Savanna had just admitted.

"Whose DNA did you use?" Devon finally asked.

"I used my own, and I did that so he would always need me. You see, since it's my DNA in his body, he needs me to keep it strong and working properly. Without me he will eventually start to reverse backwards."

"What does he need from you?" Cleo asked, although she looked as if she already knew what Savanna was going to say.

Once more Savanna looked very uncomfortable. "I only recently discovered why his cells would destroy mine. It takes blood to keep the human cells regenerating and growing. His blood, or whatever it is that he is made up of, was incompatible with it. It would break down the cells and destroy them."

"Would you like to know why it takes your blood?"

Savanna looked over at the dark-skinned woman with the colorful headwrap. "Yes, I would like to understand. Can you explain it?"

"Have you ever wondered why sacrifices require blood? Whether godly sacrifices in the Bible or satanic sacrifices, they all require blood." Cleo waited a moment to see if anyone knew the answer to her question. When everyone remained silent, she continued. "Blood *is* life. Blood contains life-giving and cleansing elements that nothing else has. So, within the blood is power. That's why the shed blood of Jesus was so powerful -- it came from the very source of life. It was enough to cleanse away every sin from every human who ever lived. When Lucifer and his minions rebelled against heaven and were cast out, they lost whatever was good and godly within them, including his life-giving blood. What he now has flowing through his veins is poison. That is why Satan demands blood sacrifices. You are giving to him what is very sacred and what he no longer has. That, dear child, is why he needs your blood for the human DNA he now carries."

"So, he needs your blood? Like a transfusion?" Sabrina asked with her brow wrinkled in confusion.

Savanna nodded. "A transfusion would work, but that's certainly not how he took it last time," she said as a small shudder went through her.

"So, he will come looking for you," Nate said.

"Without a doubt," Savanna replied.

Gideon was sure that his face expressed the same amount of shock and dismay that the other angels did. He had heard some unbelievable things during his long existence but nothing like this. The fact that it was even possible to change from demon to human was mind-blowing and, quite frankly, made him very uneasy. He asked the others what their thoughts were on the matter.

"Well, we don't have to go looking for his helper, so that's a bonus," Zareck commented with a shrug.

"Nor do we have to convince her not to help him. That's a bonus, too," Mac said.

"And we know why people have been coding and dying at the hospital," Shana chimed in.

"Yeah, so with these bonuses on the table, why do I still feel slightly ill?" Gideon asked with a rueful shake of his head.

"Probably because we know that an attack is coming."

Gideon glanced over at Kavik. "Possibly, but we have known about attacks before. Forewarned is forearmed, so that's not it."

"Is it because you don't know Savanna well enough to trust her words?"

Turning around, Gideon looked at Charlotte, who had perched herself in typical Charlotte fashion on the counter with one foot tucked under her knee.

"Do you trust her?" he asked her.

Lifting her shoulder slightly in a delicate shrug, Charlotte shook her head. "She doesn't feel deceitful, and what does she gain by telling us Karau's plans or her part in it?"

"Not to point out the obvious, but why don't we simply have Mac ask her guardian? They know her better than anyone else and can probably tell us if she is lying."

Everyone stopped and stared at Shana. "What? What did I say? Is that a dumb idea or something?" she asked, looking bewildered.

"No, that's not a dumb idea. It's a very good idea and the quickest way to probably get our answer," Gideon said with a grin.

Charlotte lifted her hand in a high-five gesture and Shana slapped it loudly.

"Girl power!" they cheered.

"Oh, brother. We will never hear the end of it," Zareck grumbled.

"Nope, and we live *forever*!" Shana smirked with a saucy little grin.

Mac leaned in to offer Zareck some words of wisdom. "Dude, don't even bother. When they team up like that, there is no winning. Just bow out gracefully."

Gideon turned to Mac, who immediately got to his feet. "I'm on it." He walked across the room to speak with the dark-haired angel in question.

Elias's dark eyes narrowed slightly as the SA angel talked with who he assumed were the other guardians. He envied the Special Assignment angel that ability. He had nodded his head at him when he had entered the room and the SA angel returned his greeting. Now he was approaching him and Elias could tell he had questions.

"Greetings, I'm Macdeveron, but everyone calls me Mac for short."

Elias took Mac's offered arm and gave it a firm squeeze. "I am Elias. I can tell that you have questions. I'm assuming that you were speaking with the other guardians?"

"Yes, naturally they have concerns about Savanna's trustworthiness. Do you think she is telling the truth about being done with her associations with demons?"

Elias turned his head and studied his human for a few long seconds before turning back to Mac. "I believe she is telling the truth as she believes it to be, at the moment."

Mac cocked his head slightly. "Sooo, what does that mean?"

"It means that she is telling the truth, that her heart is sincere in wanting to change, but Karau had a very strong hold on her. She may not be able to overcome his call."

"That's makes sense. How can we help her stay on the right path?"

Elias gave Mac a direct look. "Keep Karau away from her."

Brody hoped that no one thought him disinterested in the conversation because he hadn't asked any questions. It wasn't that he didn't have any. It was just his were more along a personal line. He was trying to recover from the shock of seeing his high school crush standing in front of them saying she was a former witch! He wished he could say he was surprised, but honestly, he wasn't. Savanna had always flirted with the dark side as she and her group of friends mocked his faith. He never understood why he always had tender feelings for the green-eyed redhead, but he did; sitting in front of her now, he was afraid those feelings hadn't changed. He also knew that she didn't recognize him when Charlie made the hasty introductions. Her eyes rested on him only for a moment before looking to the next person. That wasn't too surprising. He had been short and skinny as a rail in high school. He didn't shoot up and fill out until his college years. Now he was 6'3" and over two hundred and forty pounds, so between that and the fifteen years that had passed, he felt sure that his secret would be safe.

Cleo studied the young woman who reminded her so much of herself. She knew that Savanna would need a strong support group to resist going back to her old ways. Everyone was now standing around talking about the best the way to combat the problem and protect both the hospital and Savanna from Karau. Easing her way to the young woman's side, Cleo smiled.

"Missy, I want you to know that I understand where you are coming from better than anyone else in this room. I was deeply involved in voodoo. I was a high priestess. I can tell you right now the devil will come after you hard, and it will take more strength than you think you possess to resist him, but you can do it. Do you know why?"

"Why?" Savanna asked.

"You have the highest power there is living inside of you now. Karau and any other demon must submit to your authority. But it won't do you no good unless you believe in it." She peered closely at the woman. "Do you believe?"

"I know what I saw yesterday with Pastor Tony was unlike anything I have ever seen before. He commanded the evil spirit to shut up and it did. He commanded it to release me and come out and it did. I felt the connection between us break. I physically felt the tie break. Do you understand what I mean?"

"Oh, honey, I surely do. But you need to be really careful because that devil is a slick old thing and he will play tricks with your mind. That's why the Bible tells us that we are to renew our minds. It's in Romans." When Savanna gave her a blank look, Cleo shook her head. "The Bible is the most powerful weapon. Inside it tells you the truth of who God is, who that old devil is, and, most importantly, who *you* are. Let me go get mine. I'm just down the hall. It won't take me but a minute to go get it." Before Savanna could reply, she had turned and hurried out the door.

The next person to approach her was the man who had sat quietly while she had told her story. He had been the only one not to ask her any questions. Now he stood in front of her with a bashful smile.

"Hi, I'm Brody. I don't know if you remember…"

"Brody? Brody Miller? From high school?" Savanna's eyes grew wide as she looked him up and down, causing his face to burn.

"Well, I was going to say I didn't know if you remembered my name from when Charlie introduced me earlier, but yeah, that's me."

"Wow! You... I mean... I can't believe...Wow!" Savanna stammered as she stared at him with wide eyes.

Brody grinned as he rubbed the back of his neck nervously. "Yeah, I know I look a little different, huh? I had what you would call a delayed growth spurt."

Savanna laughed as she shook her head in wonder. "Well, I guess so! I don't think anyone would be stuffing you in trashcans or shoving your head in a toilet now."

Recalling all the horrible embarrassing things that were done to him, Brody felt his jaw muscle start to tic slightly. The sound of her laugh brought it all rushing back up to the surface. Not wanting to let her see how it still bothered him, he started to turn away, but she caught his wrist.

"I'm sorry, Brody. We were mean and horrible kids. I know that I personally said a lot of mean stuff to you. For what it's worth, I am sorry. I can't offer any excuse except I was young and stupid." He looked down into her beautiful jade eyes and felt the anger melt away. She really did seem sincere.

He gave her a soft smile. "No worries, it was a million years ago, and like you pointed out, they wouldn't do it to me now."

Savanna felt tingles go all the way to her toes at Brody's smile. He had grown so tall, filled out and was seriously good-looking. If her life wasn't so uncertain right now, she would be extremely interested in him. She quickly stopped that line of thought. He wouldn't want anything to do with her, not after the way she treated him in high school, and not after admitting everything she had been involved in. But, still, it was a nice thought, and right now nice thoughts had been few and far between for her.

Cleo hurried back with her Bible, having underlined the verse she wanted to share with Savanna. But when she saw her deep in conversation with Brody, she stood back and waited, for it didn't take any special powers to see the light of interest in both their eyes. Although she didn't know the man well, she knew enough to know that he would be very good for Miss Savanna, yes, very good indeed!

Chapter 10

Later that day after Brody and Pastor Tony took Savanna to her apartment to pick up a few things, Charlie sat with Nate and her family and tried to wrap her mind around everything she had learned that morning.

"You're awfully quiet, Charlie. Are you okay?" When Sabrina didn't get any response from her daughter, she waved her hand in front of her face. "Earth to Charlie, come in, Charlie!"

Charlie snapped her head up when she saw a hand wave in front of her face. "What? I'm sorry, did you say something?"

"Yes, I asked if you were okay. You were really lost in thought," Sabrina said with concern.

"Oh, I was just thinking about everything that Savanna told us. I guess I'm a little bit in shock. It all seems so unbelievable."

"What part do you have trouble believing, child? That she was witch or that a demon is walking around looking like a human?" Cleo asked her.

Charlie shrugged. "I guess all of it, to be honest. I knew that demons were real, but somehow, I didn't give them much thought. And when you say 'witch,' I get the image of an ugly old woman in a pointed hat flying on a broomstick like on Saturday morning cartoons. I never thought I would come face to face with one. Savanna is so pretty and looks so normal."

Cleo shook her head. "Charlie, if evil looked like what it really was, no one would have anything to do with it! Now, I'm not saying that Miss Savanna is evil, leastwise not anymore. But evil always comes wrapped in a pretty package. Look at me -- I look like any other woman you might see on the street and I was neck-deep in voodoo and the like. I have done things that would chill your blood, child."

Charlie looked somewhat taken aback at Cleo's words. "I guess I knew you were involved in that in your past, but I had almost forgotten about it. You are such a strong woman of God now that it's hard to believe you haven't always been."

"Well, I wasn't. I was just like Savanna, caught and snared up like a plump rabbit fit for the devil's frying pan. But by the grace of Almighty God I was saved and set free. People like to talk about the pretty side of Christianity. Folks getting saved and wonders and miracles and pretty angels, but far too many refuse to acknowledge the ugly side, and it's every bit as real. I guess they think that the devil and his evil cohorts stayed behind back in the Bible days. But let me tell you that he is right here in present-day America, and he is all over this world seeking whom he may devour. I know that a whole lot people are due for a very rude awakening."

"I can't believe she was able to summon that demon using a toy you can buy at your local retail store," Sabrina said with a small shake of her head. "They should be outlawed or at the very least have some sort of age requirement."

"A séance board is no toy, Sabrina, no matter how they market it. It's a powerful tool that can open doors you don't want opened. But the retailers would first have to believe it was dangerous before they would put any type of restrictions on it, and you can bet that won't happen." Cleo sighed as she rubbed her eyes. "The devil is working hard to have what used to be taboo become mainstream and acceptable or at the very least make people believe it's not real. Look at television shows that are on today. They make things like witchcraft and sorcery look fun and exciting. They lure children and even adults in with video games that make it all seem like it's harmless fun and make believe. But they are slowly and methodically planting seeds that will one day grow. We have wolves dressed up like shepherds preaching that the devil is dead and we don't have to worry about him. The churches that understand demonic warfare are few and far between. Why do you think the Bible tells us to put on the full *armor* of God? Because we are in a battle! Christians are being lulled to sleep. I fear that when the day comes, when they are called on to stand and fight, they won't be ready."

"You don't have to convince me, Cleo. After I saw how the demon in that bar influenced people, I know what they can do. But I also know what a fully-trained and prepared Christian can do, too. Being ex-military, I know that the best way to defeat the enemy is to know the enemy. People need to get their heads out of the sand and realize what is happening right in front of them."

Nate wrapped his arm around Charlie's shoulder. "I know I want both of us to be ready and prepared. I don't know much about demonic warfare but I'm sure willing to learn."

"Me, too," Charlie chimed in.

"Well, don't leave me out! If I ever run into one of those nasty things, I want to be able to send it packing!" Sabrina said with a stern look.

Cleo clapped her hands together. "All right then. Everyone, grab your Bibles. Demon Warfare Preparedness 101 is about to start!"

Gideon and the other angels all looked at one another and smiled.

Karau paced the cavern that was below the hospital with short, fast steps. His brow was wrinkled in deep thought. He had to find a way to get Savanna back under his control. It had now been three days since he had taken blood from her and he was already starting to show signs of regression. Running his tongue over his teeth, he could feel the edges starting to sharpen into points.

"Why can't we just find another to help us?"

Karau looked at the small demon who had made the suggestion. "Now why didn't I think of that? Oh, I know. It's because it's *her* blood that I need to keep me from regressing back into one of you!"

Back in the corner of the cavern another demon, named Lespar, watched Karau carefully with his blood-red eyes. The moment he had been waiting for was drawing near, but no need in wasting this perfect opportunity to sow a little discord among the brethren, so to speak.

"Back into one of us? You *are* one of us. Do you actually want to be a pathetic human with their weak bodies and short life spans? Not to mention that it seems to me you rely heavily on the help of this woman whom you have lost control over. I think your plan is failing."

Karau arched a brow at the demon who had spoken. Lespar was large and a known trouble maker, but he wasn't the smartest demon in the cave, as proven by his remark.

"I will not be fully human. I will have the best of both worlds, by appearing human but having the strength and abilities of a demon," Karau explained. "And Savanna's cooperation isn't required, only her blood. I have countless ways of ensuring that is available to me."

"So, *if* your plan succeeds, then what? Will you will think you are better than us?" Lespar goaded.

Karau crossed his arms across his chest and gave the challenging demon a disparaging look. "I know I'm better than you. What have you done to better yourself? What have you done to tip the scales in our direction? I'm not only better than you; I'm not even in the same *species* as you."

The mutterings of denial and anger could be heard whispered among the other demons. Lespar merely bowed his head to hide his smug smile.

Savanna stood and stared at her destroyed apartment. She was embarrassed for Pastor Tony and Brody to see it in such shambles. It looked as if Karau and his demolition team had been back to destroy whatever they had missed from the last time.

"I hate to break the news to you, but I think your ex has been here," Brody said as he picked up what was left of her 60-inch television. When Savanna shot him a dirty look, he feigned innocence. "I didn't say ex-what."

"You're not funny," she pointed out with a less-than-amused look as she continued to pick through what was left of her belongings.

"I'm sorry to say that it doesn't appear that he left you anything that's going to be salvageable," Tony said as he poked his head in the other rooms. "He really did a number here."

"Yeah, this isn't the first time he has thrown a world class tantrum, but I must say this is his best one." Savanna sighed as she looked around, wondering how she was going to explain this to her landlord or her insurance company. She was pretty sure this was probably not one of the things or two Farmers had covered before.

Not only had Karau destroyed all her belongings; he also did a great deal of damaged to the apartment. Huge holes dotted the walls. Light fixtures dangled on wires from the ceiling. The built-in appliances were tossed across the kitchen and food was scattered across the floor, staining the carpets. Feeling suddenly overwhelmed by everything, she sat down in the only remaining dining room chair.

"Savanna, I know it totally doesn't look like it right now, but I promise you did the right thing," Brody said as he dropped down on one knee next to her. When Savanna looked at him, the tears in her eyes and the hopeless expression on her bruised face tore at his heart.

"You're right. It really doesn't look like it right now. I can only imagine what he did to my lab."

"You have a private lab?" Tony asked.

Savanna nodded. "Yes, it was one of my 'rewards' for helping him. It was fully equipped with the latest in state-of-the-art instruments. I'm sure it's all demolished by now." Savanna's face crumpled into tears at the thought of what she had helped Karau do. Guilt rode her hard. She knew nothing she did could ever make up for it.

Not knowing what else to do, Brody pulled Savanna into his arms and held her tightly as he prayed for wisdom. He knew she had some lumps to take, but how many and how bad was yet to be determined.

Never had an embrace felt as good as the one she was currently wrapped up in. Brody's strong arms made her feel safe for the first time in a long time. She could hear him whispering against her hair. Even though she couldn't make out what he was saying, she knew he was praying for her. She could feel the tension draining from her like someone had pulled the plug in a bathtub. The irony of her situation didn't escape her. Brody Miller was the last person she would have run to for protection in high school, and now he was the one she felt the safest with. Pulling away from his embrace, she gave him a shaky smile.

"Sorry, I had a momentary break-down," she apologized.

"Hey, no worries. You are dealing with a heavy situation. I just want you to know that this isn't my first fight with the devil, and I know it's not Pastor Tony's first fight either. We will keep you safe."

"I appreciate the offer, but I don't want to be *kept* safe. I want to know how to defeat him myself," she said adamantly.

Tony placed his hand on her shoulder. "Then we shall teach you."

The man watched as the redhead he was after and two men left the apartment building and got into a blue sedan. Pulling out behind them, he stayed close enough to keep track of them but not close enough to call attention to himself. When the car pulled into the drive way of a modest brick home, he knew he had found where the woman would be staying. It was all a matter of time before he would bring her back to Karau and receive his reward.

Savanna slid deeper into the large clawfoot bathtub until her chin touched the water. The only thing she was lacking at the moment, besides everything, was some bubbles. But the steaming hot water was slowly working its magic on her tense and tired muscles. This was the first time she had been alone since Tony delivered her from Karau. The feeling was still a little surreal. Rubbing her chest lightly, she glanced up at the ceiling. She didn't know if it would be considered rude to speak to the Almighty while nude in a tub, but she was going to. Then again maybe it was better this way, stripped down with nothing to hide behind. Taking a deep breath, she started her very first prayer.

"God, I know I'm not your favorite person right now. I have done some truly wicked things that I am very sorry for. I wish I could go back in time and change what I did, but we both know I can't. Pastor Tony was telling me earlier that it didn't matter, that you loved me even while I was in my wickedness. I…I…don't see how you could, but if that is true, then I'm so grateful. Please help me stay away from Karau. Please help me to be just as strong a Christian as I was a witch. I want to follow you with my whole heart." A strong feeling of what could only be called righteous indignation started to simmer in her heart. "Help me to help others who have chosen the path I was walking. I want to teach them how evil and corrupt that lifestyle truly is."

Slamming her hand down on the side of the tub, she balled it into a fist. "I want to somehow make up for all the evil that I have done." Tears started to fall from her eyes as she bowed her head in utter shame. "I do ask your forgiveness. Wash me clean, O Lord, that I may serve you. Come into my heart and create in me a person worth dying for." With that said, she slid under the water and scrubbed her skin furiously, as if she could wash away the taint of sin from her flesh.

Tony and Brody were sitting at the kitchen table when a fresh-scrubbed Savanna joined them. Judging from the sparkle in her green eyes, more than just a typical bath had taken place in his bathroom.

"So, how are you?" Tony asked with a knowing smile on his lips.

Savanna's smile reached all the way to her eyes and across the table to Tony's heart. "I'm good… in fact, I'm better than good! I don't remember ever feeling this clean, both inside and out," she replied with a soft laugh. "I think that was the best bath of my entire life! I feel brand new. Is that crazy?"

"Not at all; in fact, it's scriptural. 2 Corinthians 5:17 says, *Therefore, if anyone is in Christ, he is a new creation. The old has passed away; behold, the new has come.* So, you are totally brand new!" Brody answered with a bright smile.

"I still find all of this so hard to believe. I can hardly take it all in!"

"It can take a little while to really sink in."

Propping her chin in her hand, Savanna smiled at Pastor Tony, "How long did it take for you?"

Faith's Legacy

"Well, I have been saved and following Jesus for more than forty-nine years and I'm still in awe of his grace every day. So maybe you don't ever get used to it," he chuckled.

"That was going to be my answer," Brody said. "I have been a follower since I was in junior high and he still totally rocks my world."

Savanna laughed at Brody's comment. "That's a pretty accurate description of how I feel. Like my whole world has been rocked on its axis."

"I imagine it does, and the closer you get to him and the more you learn who he really is by studying his Word, you will become even more rocked," Tony replied.

"That reminds me, I really need to get a Bible."

"Wait here just a moment. I will be right back." Tony jumped up from the table and went into his bedroom then emerged a few minutes later with a worn Bible in his hands. Placing it on the table, he waited for Savanna to read what was inscribed on the front.

Savanna looked up at him. "Mavery Pauline?"

Tony nodded, "Yes, that Bible belonged to my wife, but she is with the Lord now and no longer needs it. I want you to have it."

Savanna looked surprised and dismayed all at once. "Oh, no! I couldn't possibly take her Bible. You should keep it. I know it must be very special to you."

"Savanna, this Bible is special to me, but so are you. I have been holding on to it for nine years waiting for the right person to come along to give it to. The Lord spoke to my heart just a minute ago, and told me you are that person. Now, please, take it with mine and Mavery's blessing. I know she would agree."

Savanna held the Bible to her chest as tears filled her eyes. "You have given me so much. How can I ever repay you?"

Pastor Tony smiled. "Just pay it forward and help others as I have helped you."

Chapter 11

Amy sat at the foot of her husband's bed feeling completely helpless and useless. He had been in a coma for more than two weeks now. She knew the longer he was in it the less likely he was to come out of it. She had prayed until she felt like God was sick of hearing her beg, so now she sat not knowing what to do. She wished Charlie was there; she always felt much more at peace and hopeful when she was nearby. Getting up, she walked over and stared out of the window. It was now late September and the trees back home in Tennessee would be starting to change colors. But here it looked the same: tall palm trees, beautiful blue skies and the ocean. Funny, she had always wanted to see California, and now that she was here, all she could see of it was from this window. Sighing, she turned around and nearly jumped out of her skin when she saw the attractive man in a gray suit standing at the foot of Chance's bed.

"Oh! I didn't hear you come in! You startled me," she said, placing a hand over her heart.

The man smiled slightly without showing any teeth. "My apologies. You seemed lost in thought and I didn't wish to disturb you."

"It's okay. I guess I was a million miles away, well, a couple thousand miles anyway," she admitted with a sad smile.

"Missing home, are you?" the man asked.

"Yes, I am missing a lot of things right now, to be honest. So, are you another doctor? Or are you with the office of financial aid?" She looked him over and he didn't seem like the type to be either. His expensive suit and Ray Bans screamed money, but his vibe screamed Beware!

The man cocked his head slightly as he studied her. "I'm neither, actually, but I am here to help."

"How so?"

Once more he gave her a non-smile as he nodded toward Chance lying motionless on the bed. "What do the doctors say about his recovery?"

Amy shook her head. "They tell me that the longer he is in a coma, the less chance there is that he will ever wake up. Of course, it's still relatively early yet, so I still have hope."

"Do you, Amy?" he asked. "Because the woman I saw staring out of the window a few minutes ago, did not look like a woman with hope. In fact, I would say that hope was something you haven't felt in a very long time. Am I correct?"

Amy wasn't sure what startled her the most, the fact that he knew her name or the fact that he knew exactly how she was feeling.

"I am a man with some very special…let's say *skills,* and I would be very willing to give you the desire of your heart for a small favor."

"What kind of skills? Who are you?" Amy asked as her heart started to race in her chest.

The man walked to Chance's bedside and placed his hand on Chance's arm.

"Hey! What are you doing!" Amy protested and rushed to push him away. The man lifted his other hand and pointed toward the vital monitor. Amy looked and saw that Chance's blood pressure had come up, along with his oxygen level. She looked at his face and saw pink flood his cheeks and his eyelids flutter.

"He is waking up!" she cried out in joy! "Chance! Darling, can you hear me?" She watched in dismay as it all stopped as suddenly as it began. His face lost all color and his vitals dropped back to where they had been for weeks.

Then she saw that the man's hand was no longer on Chance's arm. Narrowing her eyes, she walked around the bed and stood between the man and her helpless husband.

"What did you do to him?" she asked in a firm voice.

The man shrugged slightly. "As I said earlier, I have some special skills. I can easily bring your husband back to you. All I ask is for one small favor."

"How do I know that wasn't just lucky timing? How do I know that you had anything at all to do with his sudden improvement?" Amy asked.

The man sighed then once more placed his hand on Chance's arm, and as before, all of Chance's numbers immediately improved. This time he even moaned slightly, calling her name with the softest of whispers.

"Chance! Baby, I am right here! Please open your eyes for me! Please!" But again, his face lost color and his body went still as the man stepped away.

Amy stared at the stranger who seemed to have the power of life in his hands. Could this be the miracle she had been praying for? Had God finally heard her cries?

"Are you an angel?" she asked as she looked at him in awe.

"I am much more than an angel, my dear. So, do we have a deal? You do me one small favor, and I will restore your husband to perfect health."

Amy looked back at Chance who now seemed even more pale than before. Turning back to the stranger, she asked, "What do you want me to do?"

Charlie, Nate, Savanna and Brody entered the hospital later that afternoon. They were all anxious to see if all the coding had slowed down. They were in luck when they saw Dr. Reed standing at the nurse's station.

"Dr. Reed! Hi, how are things today?" Nate asked.

The doctor smiled before answering. "Hello, Nate, the past couple of days things have been quiet. No excessive coding, no patients dying. It's been great, so whatever you're doing, it's working."

"That's wonderful news!" Charlie said with a wide smile. "I want you to meet a couple of new friends of ours. "This is Brody Miller and Savanna Becker. They will be helping us to pray over the hospital. So, if you see them around, that's why."

Dr. Reed shook hands with Savanna and Brody. His eyes lingered on Savanna's bruises, but he said nothing. "Hello, it's nice to meet both of you. Any friend of Nate and Charlie's is a friend of mine." He then looked back at Nate.

"Do you feel that this is only a lull in the activity? Do you think it's going to start again?"

Nate shook his head. "I don't know, Doc. But one thing I learned in Afghanistan is it can be a mistake to pull out too early. So, I would feel better if we hung around a few more days, if you don't mind."

Dr. Reed shook his head. "No, not at all." Then he looked up when his name was called over the intercom. "Well, no rest for the wicked or however the saying goes. It was good to see you."

After the doctor had walked on down the hall, Brody turned to Nate. "Well, where to?"

"Why don't Charlie and Savanna take this floor and me and you take the next floor up? We will meet back here in a couple of hours."

Charlie and Savanna headed for the waiting room, but before they got there Charlie saw Amy coming out of Chance's room.

"Amy! Hi, how is Chance? Is there any improvement?" Charlie asked.

The look on the young woman's face told Charlie all she needed to know before she answered.

"No, but he isn't any worse, so that's good, right?"

"That's right! Keep positive and I know he will get better. I would like you to meet a friend of mine. This is Savanna. She is a new Christian and is going to help me pray over the hospital in the waiting room. Would you like to join us?"

"Actually, I think I will take a rain check. I was just on my way out. Savanna, it was really nice to meet you." Amy smiled at them both then made her way down the hall.

"Her husband is in really bad shape, isn't he?" Savanna asked with a sad look.

Charlie nodded. "Yes, he is. He is in a coma, and the longer he stays in one the less likely the chances are that he will wake up."

"I could have killed him, too. I know for a fact that I'm responsible for the other deaths." The sorrow in her voice was easy to hear.

"You didn't kill those patients -- Karau and the other demons did," Charlie pointed out.

Savanna stopped and looked down at Charlie. She had no clue just how evil she had been.

"Charlie, it was just as much my fault because of what I was doing. Yes, I told Karau that he didn't need to kill the patients to get what he needed, but even after I knew what he was doing, I didn't stop. If I had, I could have saved lives."

"Can you change the past, Savanna? Can you spin back the hands of time and change things?" Charlie asked her.

"Of course not. Although there isn't anything I wouldn't give if I could."

"Then all you *can* do is stop him from killing anymore, and that's what you are going to do, right?" Reaching out, Charlie took Savanna's hands, squeezing them tightly. "You have asked for forgiveness and God has forgiven you. Now you need to forgive yourself. I know that's the hard part, but until you free yourself from the burden of your guilt, then you can't really move forward with your life. Look at it this way. By not accepting God's grace and forgiveness, you are basically saying that Jesus died a horrible death for nothing. He died for your forgiveness. He died so that you would not have to carry the weight of your sins any longer. Romans 6:23 states, 'For the wages of sin is death; but the gift of God is eternal life through Jesus Christ our Lord.' There isn't anything that you can do to erase your past that Jesus hasn't already done. You just need to accept it."

"It really says that?" Savanna asked in amazement.

Charlie laughed as she nodded her head. "Yes! It really does! I will write it down for you so you can find it later and read it for yourself."

"How can God love us so much? Especially when we are wicked and evil?"

Charlie thought for moment, trying to find a way to explain God's love for mankind. Finally, she smiled. "It's like this. Once when I was a young teenager I snuck out and went to a party that I wasn't allowed to go to. I ended up getting into a bit of trouble and my parents found out about it. I thought for sure that they would be so disappointed in me and wouldn't love me anymore. But they were so happy that I was brought home safe and sound that they both hugged me tightly and I could literally feel their love for me. Now I had to take my lumps for being disobedient, but I never doubted that they loved me. God is like a parent with a wayward child. He longs for us to come back home so he can get us cleaned up again and keep us safe. He is constantly calling out for his lost children, just like a shepherd will look for a lost sheep."

"I...I...think I heard him calling me," Savanna said with a wide-eyed smile of wonder. "The day that I spoke to you here at the hospital, after I left I kept hearing a soft voice call my name. I even turned around to see who it was but I didn't see anyone. It was God, wasn't it? He was trying to call me home, wasn't he?"

Charlie smiled and nodded. "After you left, I told Nate and Brody about you. I felt very much that I needed to pray for you, so we did. I think God has been calling you for a while. I'm so happy you finally heard him and came home! Now are you ready to help me pray over this hospital?"

Savanna held out her hand, "Yes, I am! Let's do this!"

Amy hurried down the hall and found a private spot to make a quick phone call. Once she had done that, she went back and tapped on the waiting room door where Charlie and Savanna were talking with a couple of other people. Pushing down the wave of guilt for what she was about to do, she plastered a bright smile on her face.

"Hi, I don't suppose I could ask you two a favor, could I?"

Charlie and Savanna both nodded. "Sure, what's up?" Charlie asked.

"I have a few things that I need to bring up from my car. I could use an extra set of arms or two."

Gideon followed behind the three women with a very bad feeling in his gut. Amy reeked of demonic influence. Whatever she was doing, he was willing to bet his left wing that it was nothing good.

They all chatted pleasantly as they rode the elevator down to the underground garage. As the elevator dropped, Gideon's bad feeling only increased.

"Charlie, don't go down there!" he whispered in her ear as the doors opened.

Savanna followed Amy then looked back to see Charlie standing very still with her head cocked to one side.

"What's wrong?" Amy asked.

"I don't know. I just got an overwhelming feeling that we shouldn't be doing this," Charlie admitted with a frown.

Amy laughed, hoping her nerves wouldn't betray her. "Don't be silly! My car is just right down this row. There are three of us going together. What could happen?"

Charlie smiled as she shook her head. "I guess you're right. One too many scary movies coming back to haunt me," she said as she stepped off the elevator.

"Nooo!" Gideon yelled to no avail. Pulling his sword, he stayed right up against Charlie. Evil was in the garage with them for every feather in his wings had now sharpened to a razor's edge. Casting his eyes everywhere, he searched for the source of his unease as the women made it to Amy's car. Amy reached and unlocked the truck then grabbed a can from inside. Turning quickly, she sprayed both Savanna and then Charlie directly in the face with the sticky foul-smelling substance, watching with tears in her eyes as they both gagged and coughed before falling lifeless to the garage floor.

Gideon felt his heart stop in his chest when Charlie's body hit the floor. The demons of influence and guilt now swarmed around Amy as she struggled to lift first Savanna and then Charlie into her trunk. The condemnation she felt was etched deep into her face.

"I'm sorry... I'm so sorry," she kept repeating over and over as she carefully closed the trunk then got into the driver's seat. He wondered as she pulled away just what Karau had promised her to make her betray Charlie's friendship like this.

Nate and Brody made their way to the waiting room to meet Charlie and Savanna.

Faith's Legacy

"Dude, I could totally eat like a whale I'm so hungry," Brody complained as he rubbed his growling belly.

Nate grinned. "Back home in Carolina we would say 'eat a horse.' but right now I could go for some whale myself."

As he entered the waiting room, his eyes swept around the room then back to Brody.

"Maybe they are at the nurse's station," Nate said as they both did an about-face and walked on down the hall. Coming to the nurse's station, they saw Sheila making some notes in the computer. Leaning against the desk, Nate smiled. "Hey, Shelia. I don't suppose you have seen my wife in the last few minutes, have you?"

"Hi, Nate. No, I haven't seen Charlie, but I just got here. I think Hattie is down the hall in room 324. Why don't you ask her?"

Taking Shelia's suggestion, the men walked down the hall and knocked softly on the room door, only opening it after they heard Hattie tell them to come in.

"Why, there is my favorite ex-patient! How are you today?" she said with a broad smile.

"Hey, Hattie, I'm good. I'm looking for Charlie; have you seen her?"

"No, not today I haven't. Did you misplace her?" Hattie teased.

Nate grinned as he nodded. "I guess I did! I'm sure she will pop up somewhere. If you happen to run into her, please let her know I'm looking for her."

"I sure will. Have you tried her cell?"

Nate groaned as he reached into his pocket. "No, because that would make too much sense, and since when did I have any of that?" he said with a self-mocking smile. Punching in Charlie's number, he waited while it rang and rang; finally, her voicemail picked up. Nate waited and then left a brief message.

"Hey, babe, we are ready to go when you guys are. Call me when you get this." Then he sent her a text saying the same thing.

"You know, bro, there aren't always signals inside the hospital. If they are in an elevator or something, you can forget it. Why don't you have her paged over the intercom?"

Nate stared at Brody in silence for a moment. "Seriously, why can't I think of stuff like that today?"

Brody gave him a bright smile. "Hey, we can't all be totally genius."

"Why don't you try Savanna's number? I'm sure they are together wherever they are," Nate said as they headed back to the nurse's station to have them paged.

Brody nodded then fished his phone from the pockets of his board shorts. After a few long seconds, he shook his head. "Nope, I got nothing. I still think the intercom will be our best bet. If they are anywhere in the hospital, they will hear it."

"Hi, still haven't found her?" Shelia asked as they walked up to the desk.

"No, not yet. Would you mind paging her over the intercom?" Nate asked.

"Sure thing," Shelia replied as she reached for the intercom button and paged both Charlie and Savanna. After fifteen minutes, had passed without hearing from either of them, she asked if she should do it again.

Nate gave Brody a worried glance before nodding his head. "Yes, please. Once more, if you don't mind."

"If they don't turn up after this one, let's go walk the hospital grounds. Maybe they stepped outside for some air," Brody suggested.

Charlie woke up in the dark, confused and disoriented, still choking and gagging on whatever it was that Amy had sprayed in her face. Unable to see anything, she patted around until she felt Savanna beside her. It wasn't until she slammed her head against something hard when she tried to sit up that she realized she was in the trunk of a car. She held still for a moment and felt the vibrations as the car took them wherever they were going. Fear exploded in her heart, causing it to race out of control as all the possible scenarios popped into her head one after another. None of them ended well. She fought hard against the urge to scream and beat against the trunk. Breathing in deeply, she tried to keep the panic at bay.

"Just focus, Charlie. Keep calm," she told herself. "God, please keep us safe. Please keep your angels around us!" she prayed.

"I'm right here, Charlie. I promise you will be safe," Gideon spoke soothingly in her ear. He didn't know any more than she did about where they were going, but he would keep his promise.

Charlie drew in a deep breath, which threw her into another coughing fit, but after a minute or two she was able to breathe well enough. She shook Savanna to wake her up. In a few minutes, she came to, coughing like crazy, much like Charlie had.

"Charlie!" she cried out.

"I'm right here." Charlie rubbed her shoulder, letting her know where she was. "We are in the trunk of a car being taken somewhere. Are you okay? Can you breathe?"

After another round of coughing and wheezing, Savanna answered, "Barely. What did she spray on us and, more importantly, why?"

"I'm afraid I don't know the answer to either question right now," Charlie admitted as she tried to roll over to get to the tail lights. She remembered watching a movie once where a person who had been tossed in a trunk was able to remove the tail light and stick an arm through the hole. She told Savanna what she was trying to do.

"Good idea! I must have watched the same movie because I remember that, too. Let me work on the other one," she said as they shifted around in the small trunk until they were both in reach of a tail light. After a few minutes and a few broken nails, they both realized that wasn't going to work.

"Maybe I can kick it out," Charlie said as she once more wiggled until she could kick at the tail light. Giving it a few hard kicks only bruised the bottom of her foot. Never in all her life had she wished more for her heavy farm boots instead of the thin-soled sandals she was currently wearing.

Panting for air in the hot and stuffy trunk, she collapsed next to Savanna and tried to catch her breath and slow her heart rate.

"Do you feel a tire iron or anything we might can use as a weapon?" she asked after she caught her breath.

"No, I'm sure there is one in here but if this car is anything like mine, it's probably under us. I don't think we can get to it," Savanna replied with a sigh. "How long do you think we were out?"

"I have no clue. I can't understand why Amy would do this to us," Charlie said with a choked whisper.

"I'm guessing it was because of me. I think you got grabbed because you were with me."

Charlie rolled her head toward Savanna. Since her eyes had grown accustomed to the dim light, she could faintly make out Savanna's profile.

"Did you know Amy? You know, from your other life?" she asked.

"No, but I bet Karau got to her. I knew he wanted me back, but I didn't think you would get dragged into it. I'm so sorry, Charlie!" Savanna's voice caught on a sob.

"Savanna..." Charlie began.

"No! Do not say this isn't my fault! All of this is my fault! I do have some responsibility here, no matter how much you say otherwise. This is the price that I have to pay for what I did. You were right -- the wages of sin is death, but my sin shouldn't be the cause of your death."

"Hey, I'm not dead yet, and neither are you. I don't know about you, but I have no intention of going out anytime soon. We just need to keep it together and be smart and wait for our chance to escape. Or if nothing else, stay alive until someone can rescue us." They both remained silent for a few minutes before Savanna asked if Charlie had thought to check for her cell phone.

"Yes, it's gone. I'm guessing Amy took it and yours, too," she answered quietly.

"Charlie?"

"What?"

"I'm scared."

"I am, too," Charlie admitted.

"At least I know that if this ends badly, I won't be going to hell." After another second, she asked, "What's heaven like? Do you know?"

"Well, I don't know the exact details, but I do know it's wonderful. I imagine it to be full of love and peace and light and joy with streets of gold and gates made from precious gems. I also think maybe it looks a lot like earth, only unspoiled and perfect, like the earth was in the beginning."

"It sounds beautiful," Savanna replied softly.

"It truly is, and as much as I love Jesus and want to see him face to face, I know that day is not today. We still have jobs to do down here," Charlie said right before they felt the car stop and the driver's side door open then shut…

Chapter 12

Nate paced the hallway of the hospital as he waited for Charlie's parents to arrive. It had now been over three hours since Charlie and Savanna had gone missing and no one had seen or heard from either of them. Both of their cell phones now went straight to voice mail, which probably meant they had been turned off.

Shana and Mac paced right along with him, both of their faces pinched with worry. Sabra, Brody's guardian, and Maxon, Pastor Tony's guardian, stood next to their humans, looking concerned as well. Mac felt slightly better when the elevator opened and Charlie's family hurried out, along with Charlotte, Zareck, and Kavik.

"Nate! Have you heard anything from them?" Sabrina asked as she rushed to his side.

"No, I haven't and no one has seen them. I think we have asked every person in this hospital a dozen times and we searched the grounds outside three times. They are not anywhere on the hospital grounds." Nate looked lost and beside himself with worry.

"What about security cameras? Has anyone looked at those?" Devon asked as he pointed to the hallway security camera in the corner.

"No, I haven't even thought about the cameras!" Nate turned and walked quickly down the hall and tapped on Dr. Reed's door. After a few minutes, he returned.

"The security department is on the next floor up. Dr. Reed has already called them and they are pulling up today's footage right now."

Ten minutes later they all stared at the small security monitor with horror as they watched Amy spray both Charlie and Savanna in the face with some unknown substance. When Charlie's body fell to the floor, Nate actually felt himself try to reach out as if he could catch her through the screen. When Amy finally got them in her trunk and shut it, Sabrina cried out softly, hiding her face against Devon's chest.

"We're going to find her. I promise we will find her. I know that God has his angels all around her." Devon spoke softly against her hair, hoping she didn't notice how his heart had tripped out of rhythm.

"I want to pray right now!" Sabrina insisted. "Everyone hold hands. We are going before the Father this instant!" Sabrina's voice was determined and full of authority as she called on everyone to pray. Even the security officers who were viewing the film with them immediately stood to their feet and joined the prayer circle.

"Jesus, I don't know where my daughter is right now, but I know that you do. You love her even more than I do, so I'm asking you to keep her safe. Place a hedge of mighty angels around both Charlie and Savanna. I want the biggest and the best that you got! So, wherever they may be, that the enemy may not be able to touch a single hair on their heads. Father, may your presence be so strong where they are that the devil cannot even stand to be near them. Give my baby girl courage and peace, Lord, and let her know…" Sabrina's voice broke briefly before she cleared her throat and continued. "Let her know that she isn't alone. We ask these things in Jesus's holy name, Amen."

Fifty miles away Gideon stood in front of Charlie in full battle mode. His body was now taller and thicker, his wings had sharpened into razors, and his sword was flaming white. The demons that filled the room and influenced Amy would have to go through him to get to Charlie! As his furious gaze met theirs, they all knew that would not be an easy task. Most, if not all, recognized who he was. He didn't know how long it would be until help arrived, but what bothered him more was the fact that he didn't know just how many more black devils would come spilling through the walls because, as skilled as he was, he had his limits. Sensing a stirring in the air next to him, he saw another angel appear. The tall male angel looked startled to see Gideon.

"You must be Savanna's guardian. I am Gideon, guardian of Charlie. The Creator must know that we have need to see one another."

Elias gave Gideon a quick glance, not wanting to remove his eyes from Savanna for even a moment.

"I am Elias. Savanna has been in danger many times during her lifetime and never has this happened, so the danger must be very great indeed."

Both Charlie and Savanna sat on the cold concrete floor with their backs against the wall, watching as Amy paced the floor with a small revolver in her hand. The place Amy brought them seemed to be an abandoned office building of some sort. They were in a room just off the garage. Once Amy had opened the trunk and instructed them to get out, she had grown increasingly worried and uneasy. Her eyes darted all around the room, jerking back to the two women on the floor only when Charlie spoke to her.

"Amy, I know you probably have your reasons, but you don't have to do this."

Amy stopped pacing and stared down at her. "Yes, I do. I'm sorry, but I do. I wasn't going to get my happy ending, Charlie. I wasn't; we both know that. Chance wasn't ever going to wake up or if he did, he wasn't going to be the Chance that I know and love."

"I don't know that, Amy, and neither do you. You don't have any idea what God's plans are for you and Chance. But I promise you this isn't going to get you what you want!" Charlie fought to keep the anger from her voice.

"Yes, it will!" Amy insisted as her eyes darted around the room once more in erratic motions. "I saw what he could do for Chance! I saw it with my own eyes! He will heal him. Make him completely whole if I help him do this one thing."

"Is this 'he' you're talking about named Karau, by any chance?" Savanna asked.

Faith's Legacy

Amy propped her hand on her hip, "Look, I don't know his name. He didn't give it, and I didn't ask. I just saw Chance start to get well whenever he placed his hands on him. He did it twice! Chance almost woke up the second time. He called my name. I'm sorry, but I love him so much! I have to give him this opportunity to get better. Don't you understand?" she pleaded.

"No, no, I don't understand and I bet Chance won't understand either!" Charlie replied. "Do you think he would want this? Do you think he would approve of your methods? You maced us and then freaking kidnapped us!"

Amy's backbone stiffened slightly as she closed her eyes briefly. "It really doesn't matter. I've made my decision. Chance will never know a thing about any of this."

"But *you* will know, Amy. Do you think you will be able to just forget about this? You're a good person, with a good heart. This will eat you until it destroys you," Charlie said softly.

"He is a demon, Amy. The man you promised to help is a demon named Karau. I know because I'm the one who made him look human. Under his pretty exterior beats the black heart of a creature straight from the pit of hell. He does nothing but tell lies and destroy lives. He had almost destroyed me, but I gave my heart to Jesus. Now even if he does take my life, he can't have my soul." Savanna stopped and rubbed her hand over her heart gently before looking back up at Amy with a sad expression. "I promise you… *I promise you*… he does not have the ability to heal your husband. All he was able to do was show you some parlor tricks to fool you into doing his bidding."

Amy shook her head. "No… no, I saw Chance get better! He called my name…he did!"

"Honey, I'm sure he did, but it wasn't Chance speaking -- it was all a trick. I know for a fact that Karau cannot heal or restore life. Only God can do that because God is the creator of life…there is no life in Karau…there is only death."

Amy held Savanna's stare for a few long seconds. Long enough to give Charlie hope that perhaps she had gotten through to her, but then her hope plummeted when the door opened and a man walked in.

Faith's Legacy

Gideon felt his wrists throb when he saw Karau. Flashbacks of intense heat and unbearable pain made him break out in a cold sweat. He knew Karau saw him, although he gave no indication. The demon only had eyes for the woman sitting on the floor next to Charlie.

Charlie didn't have to be told that the man standing before her was the demon that Savanna had just spoken of. Evil rolled off him in waves so thick that it made her heart pound painfully and her tummy hurt. Clearly, he needed Savanna's help very badly because he seemed to be losing his human appearance in places. Patches of black leathery skin could be seen on his scalp, face and hands. Three fingers were tipped with black talons where human fingernails should be, and when he smiled, he smiled with a mouthful of razor-sharp teeth. Reaching over, she quickly grabbed Savanna's hand as she whispered the name of Jesus under her breath.

Karau paused as he felt the power of God wash over him, making his skin burn and his eyes tear up. "Shut her up," he ordered the demon who was currently controlling Amy. Charlie watched in horror as Amy's eyes turned white. She lifted the gun and pointed it right at her chest.

"Karau! Stop! I swear if you hurt her, I will not help you!" Savanna yelled out as she threw herself in front of Charlie, trying to protect her.

Amy walked closer in a stiff-legged fashion until she was less than three feet away. The click of the hammer cocking echoed loudly in the room. Gideon leaped into action. When he thrust his sword into the woman's body, the demon inside screamed, although to Charlie and Savanna it was as if Amy herself screamed, doubling over as if in great pain. The gun dropped, sliding across the floor, coming to rest against Savanna's foot. Reacting quickly, she grabbed it and in a move that no one saw coming, she placed the barrel of the gun to her own temple.

Back at the hospital Devon pulled a very distraught Nate to the side to speak with him privately before the police arrived on scene.

"Nate, I know how worried you are. I am, too, but you're not doing Charlie any good by letting your emotions control you. I need you to do what you were trained to do. If you were back East right now and someone of great importance was kidnapped, what would you do first?"

Nate's dark brown eyes held Devon's serious gaze and for a moment anger rolled over him hard and fast until he realized the man was right. He was letting his emotions get in the way of what needed to be done. Taking a deep breath, he squared his shoulders.

"I would find out everything I could about the suspect," he answered in a steady voice.

Devon nodded in approval. "Good, what do we know about this woman, Amy?"

"Her husband was seriously wounded and is a patient in this hospital. From what I have heard, he isn't responding well to treatment and is still in a coma. I know that Charlie has been talking and praying with Amy."

"So, what would make her do something like this? It seems as if Charlie and Amy were friends," Devon commented.

"It wasn't Charlie Amy was after; it was Savanna. Our Charlie just happened to be there."

Nate and Devon looked at Cleo, who had walked up next to them.

"You know I'm right," she insisted.

Devon nodded. "I think you probably are. Now the next question would be why does Amy want Savanna?"

Cleo cocked her head as she stared up at Devon with an impatient look. "Boy, it ain't Amy that wants her! It's that nasty demon. You two have got to stop looking at this fight from the physical side. This is a spiritual fight. Karau is likely in need of more of Savanna's blood, so he promised Amy something tempting enough to get her to lure Savanna down to the basement. Charlie just happened to be with Savanna at the time, so Amy had to take both of them. Now if I was guessing, I would say that he promised Amy that he would make her husband well. I can't think of anything else that would make her do something like this. Fear of losing someone you love is a great motivator."

Nate and Devon stared down at her in surprise. "You ever consider going into law enforcement?" Nate asked with a slight smile, which was all he was capable of producing at the moment.

Cleo shook her head. "You men always thinking with your heads," Cleo tapped the side of her head with her finger, "when you should be thinking with your heart!" She reached out and jabbed each man with the tip of her finger in the chest right over their hearts.

"Okay, so let's say that's the reason," Devon paused when Cleo raised her eyebrow at him, "and it most likely is. We still don't know where she took them."

Cleo nodded. "That's true enough, but you got to remember one thing."

"What's that?" Nate asked.

"Our girl isn't alone. She has her guardian with her and I know he will keep her safe!"

Charlie stared in horror at Savanna as she held the barrel of the gun firmly against her temple. "Savanna, what are you doing?"

"Yes, what *are* you doing?" Karau asked with a deep frown.

"I know it's me that you want, and I know that you don't need me to be willing. All you need is for me to be alive. I'm not scared to die anymore. I know my soul will go to heaven and you will be left with no one to help you or provide what you need. It's the easiest solution."

"We can defeat him without you taking your own life, Savanna! There is another way," Charlie pleaded. She glanced over to where Amy was now a huddled mess on the floor, groaning and crying. She was speaking but making no sense. Charlie turned back to Savanna, who appeared calm and in control of her actions. That scared Charlie even more than Amy's current condition.

With tears filling her beautiful green eyes, Savanna shook her head. "No, this is the only way I know he won't be able to use me.

This is how I fix what I have done. Truly, I'm not scared at all. Thank you, Charlie, for everything." Closing her eyes, she tightened her finger on the trigger.

In the brilliant light of the muzzle flash two things happened almost simultaneously. Something jerked the gun away from Savanna's head and pointed it at Karau and then both Charlie and Savanna were shoved away from the force of the blast.

Karau's face had a stunned and slightly perplexed expression as green fluid dripped from between his fingers as he clutched his chest. Dropping to his knees, he stared hard at Savanna, his black eyes promising retaliation, before they slid closed and he fell face first onto the concrete floor. The human flesh quickly started to dissolve. When Karau's true form emerged, he found himself pinned to the wall by Gideon's sword. Black demon flesh sizzled, as it encountered the holy light that illuminated the weapon. Gurgling and choking on green fluid, he eyed Gideon with hatred that ran so deep he gagged on it.

"You know I will be back," he promised as he writhed in agony on the length of Gideon's sword.

Shoving his sword in to the hilt, Gideon stared down at him. "And you know I will be right here, waiting for you."

Without another sound Karau faded away...

Chapter 13

Charlie placed a trembling hand over her heart to make sure it was still beating. Savanna sat up and shook her head slightly as she looked around.

"What just happened?" she asked as she looked around the room.

Charlie shook her head as she slowly got to her feet. "I have no idea! One second you had the gun to your head pulling the trigger; in the next, someone knocked it away from you and aimed it at that...that...whatever he was! Next thing I knew, we were both on the ground and it was dead on the floor." Charlie looked over to where Karau had been standing less than two minutes ago. All that was left was a dark stain on the concrete and hunks of human flesh that were quickly dissolving away. The sound of muffled sobbing could be heard coming from Amy, who was still lying on the floor in a heap. Charlie hurried over to her.

"Amy? Are you okay? Are you hurt?" she asked as she stroked her hair away from her tear-soaked face. Amy looked up, her eyes filled with self-hatred.

"I'm so sorry! You were right...he was a monster! How did I ever fall for his lies? I'm so ashamed!" She buried her face in her arms, unable even to look at Charlie, so great was her shame.

Savanna came over and sat down cross-legged on the floor next to Amy. She reached out and tapped Amy's shoulder.

"Hey, at least you did what you did for the person you love. I helped him for a purely selfish reason. I understand why you did it, Amy, and I can only speak for myself, but I hold no hard feelings toward you. Karau was very good at what he did. He caught you at a weak moment and offered to restore the health of your husband. Very few people would be able to refuse that."

Amy raised her head and looked up at Savanna in surprise. "Really? You seriously don't hate me? But I almost got you killed!"

Savanna smiled as she nodded. "True, but make no mistake -- Karau would have found a way to get to me sooner or later. He wasn't going to forget about me. As you could tell by his appearance, he was already starting to regress back into his real form. Now it's over, at least until he regroups. He may always come after me, but that's a reality I will have to face on my own. I know now that God will always have my back, and when my time comes, I can face death with no fear of what is beyond this life. So, for that I thank you."

"I don't understand. What are you thanking me for?" Amy asked with a puzzled look.

"You may not have seen what happened, but something, and I'm guessing it was an angel, knocked the gun away from Savanna and pointed it toward Karau. Then we were both pushed away from the force of the blast. God showed up here today in a way I never seen before. Now that I'm not scared to death, I'm actually amazed!" Charlie said with a wide smile.

Savanna matched her smile with one of her own. "It was the coolest thing I have ever seen, too, and I have seen some things in my lifetime. But *nothing* like what just happened!"

Amy looked over at Charlie. "Charlie? Can you ever forgive me? I really will understand if you can't. I know I don't deserve it."

Pulling Amy into a tight hug, Charlie laughed. "Of course, I forgive you. Like Savanna pointed out, you were in a very vulnerable position. Karau played on your biggest fears. Besides, we're fine, no harm done, and look at what a testimony we have now! Wow! I hope everyone believes us." Charlie slapped both hands to her face. "Oh, my gosh! Nate must be out of his mind with worry and my folks, too. Amy, where is my cell phone? I have to call them right now."

Amy quickly got to her feet. "They are in my car. Come on; you can call them while I drive you back."

Elias and Gideon flew next to the car as they quickly made their way back to the hospital after Charlie had spoken to a very relieved Nate.

Elias reached out and tapped Gideon's shoulder to get his attention.

"So, what made you think to shoot Karau?"

Gideon shrugged. "Well, it suddenly occurred to me that if our weapons wouldn't work on him because he too human, that maybe human weapons might work. I didn't know for sure if it would work, but it was the only thing I could come up with at the time."

The other angel smiled as he held out his fist for a "fist bump." "Now I know why you are the commander. Very good work, sir, very good indeed."

As they made their way back, Gideon couldn't help but feel that they had not seen the last of Karau...

Sabrina watched for Amy's car anxiously. All she wanted to do was wrap her arms around Charlie and never let her go. Never had she been so scared in all of her life and prayed that she would never experience anything like this again. Devon wrapped his arm around her shoulders.

"I know what you're thinking, but you can't wrap her up in bubble wrap and lock her in her room."

Sabrina raised a brow at him. "Oh, can't I?" Her brave words were followed by a deep sigh. "I know I can't. I also know that just like today, God can protect her far better than I can, but I still can't help but want to lock her away somewhere."

Squeezing her tighter, Devon let out a deep sigh of his own. "I know. I would be lying if I said I didn't feel the same way."

Amy's car pulled into view. Before it had made a complete stop, the passenger door was flung open as Charlie leaped out and ran into Nate's arms. He lifted her off her feet and held her tighter than ever.

"Oh, baby, I thought I would never see you again!" he said, his voice thick with emotion.

"I know. I was scared, too, but Nate, wait until I tell you everything that happened! You're not going to believe me but it's all true! God showed up and...and...Nate?"

Nate's attention was now riveted on the woman who was slowly getting out of the driver's seat. Nate's face grew flush with anger as he gently set Charlie aside.

"Nate, wait... let me explain! Nate!" Charlie pulled hard on Nate's arm but she didn't even slow him down as he quickly approached Amy, who stood frozen in fear by her car.

Savanna pushed herself in front of Amy, just as Nate reached her.

"Nate, stop. Listen, it's okay, really," she insisted.

Nate's brown eyes clashed with hers. "No. It most certainly is *not* okay. I don't care what her excuse or reason was for what she did! **It will never be okay**!" he roared as he tried to reach around both Charlie and Savanna to get his hands on Amy.

Devon and Pastor Tony quickly intervened, grabbing both of his arms, and hauled him back a few steps.

"Nate, let's all take a deep breath and try to calm down," Tony said as he held his arm tightly.

Nate jerked his arm out of Tony's grasp. "Let me go," he hissed through clenched teeth. When Devon grabbed for his arm, Nate held it out of his reach. "I'm okay... just give me a few minutes alone with my wife and get *her* out of my sight," he growled.

Savanna took Amy's arm and quickly led her inside the hospital to give Nate some space. Catching Pastor Tony's eye, she motioned for him to follow them.

Sabrina finally got to hold her daughter once Nate had calmed down. Cupping Charlie's face in her palms, she stared firmly into her eyes.

"Charlotte Marie, I have never been so scared in all my life!"

Charlie hugged her mama tightly. "I'm so sorry, mama. I was really scared, too, but just wait until I tell you what happened!" Charlie's words were drowned out by the sound of the police sirens as they came swooping into the hospital parking lot.

"Oh, no. Who called the police?" Charlie asked in dismay.

"Who called them? Who do you think? You had just been kidnapped!" Nate said in disbelief.

"But I'm not pressing charges and neither is Savanna. It was all a misunderstanding," Charlie protested.

Nate stared down at her, unable to even comprehend what she was saying. "A misunderstanding? I watched her spray something in your face, then I saw your body hit the ground, and *then* I watched, unable to do anything, while she loaded you into her trunk and left! That's not a misunderstanding -- that is kidnapping in the first degree!"

Charlie propped her fists on her hips. "Nate Jackson, I know what happened. I was there, remember? But you haven't heard her side of the story. If you would just calm down and listen to me, you would understand!"

Two officers approached. "I'm Officer Griggs and this is Officer Spencer. We received a call about a kidnapping. Is that correct?"

"Yes!" Nate answered.

"No!" Charlie answered just as quickly.

The officers looked at them with stern expressions. "Look, it's against the law to file a fraudulent report. So, was there a kidnapping or not?"

"I'm sorry, officer. My husband saw something that made him believe I was kidnapped, but as I have been trying to explain," Charlie shot Nate a hard look, "it wasn't like that."

Officer Griggs looked at Nate. "What did you see that made you believe your wife had been kidnapped?"

Nate glanced at Charlie who was silently begging him with her eyes not to tell the whole story. With a small shake of his head, he faced the officer.

"Sir, my wife is telling the truth. As you can see, she is safe and sound, so I clearly was mistaken. I am sorry for bothering you with this."

Officer Spencer eyed both Charlie and Nate for a long moment before he put his pen and notepad back into his pocket.

"That's fine. I wish all reported kidnappings ended like this." Then they both nodded and got back in their patrol car.

Charlie heaved a sigh of relief when the police car drove out of sight. "Thank you. I thought for sure you were going to have Amy arrested."

"I'm still not convinced that I shouldn't," Nate replied.

"Why don't we find Savanna and all go back to the hotel so Charlie can tell us the whole story? Then maybe this entire mess will make some sense," Cleo suggested.

Savanna and Tony sat with Amy in the small chapel inside the hospital. The poor woman looked utterly distraught and defeated.

Faith's Legacy

Quickly Savanna explained to Tony why Amy had done what she did and the outcome. He looked at her with understanding.

"Dear girl, while I cannot condone your actions, I can understand why you did it. I understand the fear you feel at the thought of losing your spouse. I lost my wife a few years ago."

"I don't know how you did it. I can't even stand the thought of losing Chance…I can't! He is my entire world," Amy said, the fear and heartbreak easily heard in her voice.

"I felt the same way. I was also very angry with God for allowing something as devastating as cancer to happen to someone as sweet and good as my Mavery."

"Well, it looks as if you came to terms with it, and I bet you didn't make a deal with the devil to try to save her," Amy replied.

Tony shrugged slightly. "I was never offered a deal, so who is to say that I wouldn't have taken it? I would like to say that I wouldn't have, but when the cancer had ravaged her down to less than a hundred pounds and she was so weak that she couldn't even take a deep breath, who is to say that I wouldn't have grabbed on to any chance to save her?"

"But you're a man of God. Didn't you have faith that God would heal her?"

"At first I had all the faith in world. I never thought for one second that she would die from the cancer. I fully expected her to recover and have a wonderful testimony, but that's not what happened."

Amy wiped tears from her eyes. "How did you survive after…after she wasn't here anymore?"

"By God's never-ending grace. There were days when all I could do was lie in bed and weep, but you know what? God was right there weeping with me. He knew and understood the heartache I was feeling."

"Why didn't he heal her? If he didn't answer your prayers, what hope do I have that he will answer mine?" Amy asked with a choked sob.

"Because his answer to your prayer may not be the same answer that was mine. Amy, I can't tell you why God allows some to stay and not others. That isn't for us to understand. It's our job to trust in his decision. That's not always an easy thing to do, and he understands that. That's why when I had no faith, no hope, no reason to trust him, he held me even tighter. Whatever answer he gives, know that you won't have to face it alone."

"I'm scared...I'm so scared, Pastor! Sometimes I think that Chance can sense my fear and it might make him fearful. I don't want that. I don't know what to do. It seems that all I can do is make horribly wrong choices."

"That's because you're not letting God make the choices, Amy. You need to put Chance in God's hands and leave him there -- stop getting in the way. Step aside and let God work." Tony paused as he gave Amy a long, thoughtful look. "Tell me, child, have you accepted Jesus?"

Amy gave him a startled look. "I...I believe in Jesus and in God; is that what you mean?"

Tony shook his head. "No, there is a difference in believing and accepting. Even Satan believes in him. I'm asking, have you asked Jesus into your heart? Have you asked him to cleanse you of your sins and to guide you through this life?"

Amy lowered her head as she shook it. "No, I haven't done that at all."

"Would you like to?" Tony asked softly.

Amy nodded her head quickly. "Yes, yes, I would. Can you help me?"

Savanna stepped forward with a smile and took her hand. "We both will."

Gideon and Shana followed Nate and Charlie as they went inside the hospital to look for Savanna. Nate was clearly still very upset and angry with Amy, which Gideon understood. He was none too pleased with her himself, but he also knew what she had been up against, so he had insight into the situation Nate didn't have. He thought that perhaps Mac might fill him in when they got a chance to speak privately. His wings still felt twitchy, and he had a very uneasy feeling that this wasn't over.

"So, do you have a bad case of the twitches, too?" Zareck asked as he walked up beside him.

Gideon nodded. "Yes, I do. I know that Karau himself may be out the picture for a while, but I think there is still another shoe to drop. I just don't know from where."

"We better stay close and tell the others to stay close as well. Mac needs to tell Nate to be exceptionally watchful over Charlie. If I was him, I wouldn't let her out of my sight."

Gideon gave Zareck a rueful grin. "I think that's his plan, but you can bet that Charlie will fight him sword and dagger over it. She hates being babied, and that's exactly how she will take it."

"Perhaps if she thought it was her idea, she might be more accepting of it," Kavik suggested as he joined the conversation.

Zareck arched a blonde brow. "Why would that matter?"

Kavik and Gideon just looked at one another and exchanged smiles.

Chapter 14

Karau slowly and painfully made his way back down into the cavern under the hospital. His entire plan was crumbling apart and he had that witch to blame! Hatred burned and rolled in his stomach, adding to his discomfort. He wasn't finished with her or the rest of that group, not by a long shot. Once he recovered he...

Lespar brought the sword down across the back of Karau's neck with all his might, watching as his severed head rolled across the dirt, stopping only when it bounced against another demon's leg. Hisses and curses could be heard as the others in the room looked at him with morbid speculation. Lifting Karau's severed head up with the tip of his sword, Lespar walked around the room slowly, letting every demon there get a good look.

"Karau was weak! Karau depended upon a *human*," he spat out the word, "to help him achieve his goals." Flinging the head against the wall, he held each demon's stare in turn as he walked the room.

"I am now your leader. Do any challenge me?"

The room was silent except for the sound of nervous shuffling. Lespar's thin lips stretched into a small smile.

"I thought not."

Nate sat in stunned silence along with the others as they listened to Charlie and Savanna recount their harrowing experience. Amy sat silently, as far away from Nate as she could get and still be in the same room. He didn't blame her. Now that he had heard the entire story, he somewhat understood her motives, although that did not excuse them. Looking at Charlie, he wondered what he would do if he were in Amy's position. What if it was his wife upstairs in that bed with little hope of recovery? What lengths would he take to ensure her return? It was a sobering thought and for the first time he felt a pang of sympathy for the woman.

Excusing himself, he got up and went out into the hallway. He needed some time alone to try and process what he felt the Lord was telling him. He wasn't quite ready to forgive Amy for what she did. Every time he closed his eyes, he could still see Charlie's body falling to the ground. Never had he known fear like he did in that moment. Not during battles overseas with bullets flying over his head, not while the helicopter was falling to the ground and bursting into flames. Not even during his recovery when he fully realized the true extent of his injuries. He literally felt his heart seize up with cold terror when he watched Amy's car pull out of the garage with Charlie locked in her trunk. Mac shimmered into view next to him with a look of concern on his face.

"Are you all right?" he asked. When Nate looked up at him with tears in his eyes, Mac knew that Nate most definitely wasn't all right. Putting his hand on Nate's shoulder, he guided him down the hall to an empty room where they could speak privately. Once he had slipped inside, he unlocked the door so Nate could come in.

"Do you want to talk about it?" he asked. Nate shook his head as he sat down in a chair then doubled over as he covered his face and wept. Harsh, ragged sobs tore up from his soul as he released the fear and the anguish he had kept locked inside all day.

Mac shook his head in sympathy as he knelt next to Nate and wrapped his arms around him. He offered no words of solace. Right now, Nate needed to purge the poison from his heart. After a few minutes, the sobs eased up. Mac handed him a box of tissue that Nate took with a watery smile.

"Thank you, but if you ever tell anyone I lost it like this, angel or not, I'm kicking your butt."

Mac grinned. "As if, human. But no worries. Your secret is safe with me. You had every right to 'lose it.' What you went through today was extremely scary."

Nate nodded as he played with the wadded tissue in his hand. "I thought I had lost her, Mac. I really thought I had lost her." He looked up at Mac. "How would I have dealt with it if I had? Charlie is my world, my everything. I can't not have her with me. I swear I'm never letting her out of my sight again," he vowed.

Mac sighed as he leaned against the wall and gave Nate a speculative look.

"What? Why are looking at me like that?" Nate asked.

"I'm debating with myself, that's why," Mac answered.

"Debating about what?"

"I'm debating whether to tell you something, and just exactly how much trouble I will get into if I do."

"Is it something about Charlie?"

Mac nodded. "It's about Charlie's guardian, actually. I'm wondering if you knew who it was if that would ease your mind."

Nate's eyes widened. "Well, you have to tell me now. You can't just lead in with a statement like that without finishing it."

"I know, but you have to promise that you will never tell Charlie or anyone else. This is for your ears only so you won't worry so much about her and make her nuts by keeping her locked away somewhere trying to keep her safe."

"I promise," Nate agreed as he lifted one hand in the air.

"Okay, as you know, everyone has a guardian, but Charlie's is not your average guardian angel. In fact, he isn't a *guardian* angel at all."

"He isn't? Then what is he?" Nate asked with a confused look.

"He is a warrior angel and not just any warrior angel either. He is the lead commander over all the heavenly warriors in God's army. But he was pulled off his regular duties and assigned to guard Charlie."

"Why?"

Mac shrugged. "I really don't know. All he told me was that he had to guard Charlie because she would save someone very dear to the Lord. So, Charlie has the best, toughest angel there is. He will protect her always, of that you don't have to worry. In fact, he was the one who redirected the gun and shot Karau. He is smart and will stop at nothing to keep her safe. He loves her very, very much."

Nate's eyes grew even wider. "Wow... I guess she is in very capable hands, then, isn't she?"

"Absolutely, so try to remember that when you feel the urge to wrap her in bubble wrap," Mac said with a chuckle.

"So, how do I get past this anger I feel for Amy? Do you have any secret methods for that?" Nate asked with a pained expression.

Faith's Legacy

Mac shook his head. "Afraid not, but I do know this. The Lord promises to help us in all things, so why don't you ask him to help you to forgive Amy?"

Nate nodded then bowed his head and did exactly what Mac had suggested.

A few minutes later Nate came back into the room with the others. Clearing his throat, he walked over to sit next to Amy on the couch. He offered her a smile and placed his hand gently on her arm when she tried to get up.

"Amy, please, wait. I would like to offer my apologies."

Amy watched him warily as she eased back down in her seat. "No apologies are needed, Nate. I'm the one who needs to apologize to *you*! I don't blame you one bit for wanting to wring my neck. I would feel the same way. All I could see was a way to bring Chance back to me. I was selfish and didn't even consider what it might mean for Savanna and Charlie, although Karau did say he wouldn't harm her. He said he only needed to speak with her." Amy sighed as she looked down at her hands where she twisted her wedding band nervously. "But I knew he was lying. I just didn't care. What kind of person does that make me? Charlie has been nothing but kind to me and a true friend. I could have let Charlie go and only taken Savanna, but I was scared that Charlie might interfere." Amy's face crumpled as she turned her head away and sobbed. Astonishingly, Nate felt an overwhelming need to comfort the woman that only minutes ago, he would have loved to toss into a jail cell forever, but now he pulled her into his arms and held her as she cried. He prayed for forgiveness, for himself and Amy. He prayed for her husband and he prayed that God would use their miracle for his glory.

The angels all watched as a miracle quietly happened. Nate's heart was softened and Amy's heart was mended.

Later that night Nate held Charlie tightly after they had turned out the lights. Even knowing what he did about her guardian, he was still tempted to lock her up somewhere.

"Babe, I can't breathe." Charlie's muffled voice jerked him from his inner musings.

"I'm sorry, sweetheart. I told myself I wouldn't hang on to you too tightly but I guess I lied." Shifting, he rolled over so he could see her face. Running his fingertips over her cheeks, he marveled once more how he managed to marry someone so beautiful. He let his eyes drift over her upturned nose and rose petal lips. Finally, he looked into her eyes. They were studying him curiously but with understanding.

"I'm sorry," she whispered.

"This wasn't your fault. I don't think you had any choice," Nate replied.

"Actually, I did." Charlie took a deep breath then flipped over to her back and stared at the ceiling.

"What do you mean?"

"I mean that before I stepped off the elevator I had a very strong feeling that I shouldn't. I even commented to Savanna that maybe we shouldn't."

Nate's eyes narrowed slightly as he looked at her. "What did Savanna say?"

"She didn't say anything. Amy laughed and asked what could happen, that her car was right there and there were three of us, so we would be safe. I never dreamed that it was Amy I needed to fear," Charlie said with a slight shudder.

"Oh, baby, you must have been scared out of your mind. I'm so sorry." Nate pulled her snuggly against him and rubbed her shoulders.

"I was scared; I can't deny that. But somehow, I knew I would be okay. I felt as if God was right there with me. Of course, I prayed like crazy, but I have never felt such an intense presence of God as I did in that trunk."

"Well, it was a tight space," Nate teased to make her smile. His gamble worked and she grinned.

"You have no idea. I have never been claustrophobic but I totally understand the feeling now."

"Do you think you can do me a favor?" Nate asked as he cupped her jaw and pulled her closer.

"Yes," Charlie whispered.

"The next time you get an overwhelming feeling you shouldn't do something...please, don't do it."

Charlie could only nod her answer as Nate had leaned in and captured her lips in a sweet kiss that told her everything his words could not.

Savanna sat in Tony's car and waited while he spoke to a few members of his church that had been at the hospital visiting a friend. Now that her adrenalin had worn off, the stress of the day was crashing down on her pretty hard. Covering a jaw-cracking yawn with her hand, she jumped when Brody tapped on her window. He gave her an apologetic smile when she rolled down the window.

"Hey, sorry. Didn't mean to startle you."

"It's okay. I'm sure I'm jumpier than usual," she replied with a small smile.

Brody nodded as he looked around the parking lot then back to Pastor Tony then around the parking lot again. If Savanna didn't know better, she would say he was nervous.

"Brody? Did you want something?" she asked.

He rubbed the back of his neck then nodded. "Yes, I mean, it's probably too soon or something, and I don't want you to feel...you know, like you have to or anything..."

Savanna interrupted his rambling. "Dude, you're like...stammering."

Hearing Savanna use his lingo made him stop and grin at her. "You're totally right. So, here is the deal. I like you. I always have. Do you think you might want to go out sometime?" He said the words in a rush then waited in agony when she turned her head and looked out the windshield.

"Yes, I would like that," she answered softly.

"You would? Really?" Brody asked in surprise.

Savanna nodded as she smiled up at him.

Amy sat alone in her husband's dark hospital room with a heavy heart. She desperately needed someone to talk to but she didn't know who. No one would understand what she had done. She didn't even understand it. Guilt was a tangible thing in her heart now. Sighing deeply, she leaned back in the chair and stared up at the ceiling tiles.

"God? Are you there?" she whispered. Even after accepting Christ into her heart earlier, she still wasn't sure how this worked. Charlie's family made it look so easy. They talked to God and about God like he was another member of their family.

"That's because he is."

Amy whipped her head around. "Who said that? Who is here?" she asked as her heart thudded painfully in her chest. What if it was another demon coming in to make deal? She sent up a hasty prayer for protection and wisdom.

"I'm sorry. I thought you heard me come in. The name is Mac; I'm just here to clean up a little bit."

Amy studied the old man with silver hair and large, kind brown eyes. She couldn't recall ever seeing him before, but he was pushing a custodial cart and seemed to know his way around the room, even in the dim lighting. She felt her heart rate begin to slow down.

"It's okay. I was just lost in my own thoughts," she narrowed her eyes at him, "although you seemed to know what I was thinking."

Mac shrugged as he emptied a waste basket into the larger one in his cart. "When you have been around as long as I have, Miss, you can usually tell what someone is thinking by their expressions. I guessed that you were wondering about God and where he was in all of this. Am I right?"

Amy nodded. "You hit it right on the head. You see, my friend Charlie and her family make talking to God seem so easy. I'm sorry. You probably don't know who I am talking about."

Mac stopped sweeping long enough to nod his head. "Oh, I know Miss Charlie and her husband Nate, along with the rest of her family, fine Christian folks. They got a real strong faith in God."

"Yes, yes, they really do. Anyway, I've only recently accepted Christ and..."

"Why, that's wonderful!" Mac broke in with a brilliant smile. "That's the best thing a person can do. I have never known a single person that has ever regretted making that decision, and I've known a lot of people in my lifetime." Mac leaned on his broom and beamed at Amy.

Amy blinked a couple times trying to find her train of thought once more. There was something very...*odd* about this custodian. She had never seen anyone so happy pushing a broom and dumping waste baskets. Joy seemed to seep right out of his pores and shoot out through his eyes to infect whoever was in close contact with him. She could feel it bubbling up in her own heart. Smiling, she nodded happily.

"Yes, it truly is wonderful, but I'm just a little lost on how to establish my relationship with him," Amy admitted.

"You know, the best way to really get to know someone is to read their diary; they write every thought, every dream, every hope in there," Mac replied with a wink.

Amy laughed softly. "Well, that would be really intrusive, and besides I don't have God's diary, although it would be really nice if I could know all of that about him."

"Actually, you can read it and, more importantly, he wants you to. It's all right here. Everything you could ever want to know about God is written right here in his Word. He doesn't keep it hidden away or locked up." Mac reached inside his cart and pulled out a Bible, placing it in Amy's lap. The cover was glossy black, the pages edged with gold. It was so beautiful that Amy stroked the cover with awe.

"I have never thought of the Bible as God's diary before, but I guess you're right. He has written his innermost thoughts and hopes for us inside. I remember that much from Sunday school." She started to hand the Bible back to Mac when he shook his head.

"No, ma'am, that's yours to keep. I have more at home," Mac insisted.

Tears glistened in Amy's eyes as she held the Bible to her chest like a precious treasure. "Thank you, Mac."

Faith's Legacy

"I would suggest starting with the 91st Psalm. Then I would read the four Gospels: Matthew, Mark, Luke and John. By then you will have a good idea about Jesus and how he feels about you." Mac turned his cart toward the door to leave when Amy jumped to her feet and stopped him with a hand on his arm.

"But how do I pray? How do I talk to God like he is in the room the way Charlie does?" she asked.

Mac chuckled. "You just did it. You open your mouth and you speak words, but the most important part of praying isn't about talking." He tapped his ear with one finger, "It's about listening."

After Mac left, Amy turned on a small light and opened the Bible to the 91st chapter of Psalms. Reading it slowly, she felt for the first time that she had an inside track to knowing the heart of God, and she couldn't help but smile at the thought that it came from the most unlikely of sources.

Chapter 15

Charlie knocked on the door to Chance's room. She hoped that Amy was there. She wanted to speak to her and to see how Chance was doing. After hearing Amy's voice say to come in, she opened the door to find her sitting near a window with a Bible open in her lap. Amy smiled at her and waved her into the room.

"Charlie! Hi, look what someone gave me! Isn't it beautiful?" Amy said, holding up the Bible for Charlie to see.

Charlie took the Bible, feeling the familiar and always comforting weight of it in her hand. "It's very nice. Who gave it to you?"

"You're not going to believe me, but it was a custodian. His name was Mac, and just the nicest person you could ever meet. He told me that this was like God's diary, and it was the best way to get to know him. Isn't that a cool way of putting it?"

Charlie's eyes grew wide at the mention of Mac's name. She hadn't thought about her old friend or seen him, for that matter, since they had been here.

"It is a neat way of looking at the Bible; if nothing else, it appeals to the nosy side of human nature. I know Mac, and you're right -- he is very nice. He was probably the one who held me together the most when I was here with Nate, but I haven't seen him since we have been back. I thought perhaps he moved away or quit. I will see if I can find him now that I know he is still around. I would love to see him again," Charlie replied as she returned Amy's Bible.

"Last night was the first time I have seen him, so maybe he just fills in as needed? But if I see him again, I will get his phone number or find out when he works next so you can get together."

"Thank you, I would appreciate it. So, how are you?" Charlie asked as she sat down.

The smile on Amy's face told Charlie she was doing much better before her words could.

"I'm good, better than good, actually. I have been reading the scriptures that Mac suggested and I can't believe how much peace

I have now. It's really remarkable! I honestly feel like God is here with me, right in this room," she said with a laugh.

Charlie nodded. "I know. It's hard to understand unless you experience it. It doesn't seem to matter what I am going through -- when I pick up my Bible, I find my peace and a scripture that speaks to my situation every time!"

The room grew silent as each woman reflected on her current situation.

"Amy."

"Charlie."

They both tried to speak at the same time then laughed.

"Go ahead," Charlie insisted with a smile.

"I was just going to say how thankful I am that God brought you into my life, and I know without a doubt that he did, although you may not feel the same way after yesterday."

"Of course, I feel the same way. I could have lived without being maced in the face and tossed in a trunk. I'm not going to lie about that, but what's important is the end result and that made every discomfort worth it. Besides, if that's the worst thing that ever happens to me as a Christian, I'm getting off easy. Christians in the Bible and even today are being killed for their faith."

Amy's eyes grew wide in horror. "Right now? In modern times Christians are being killed?" she asked in disbelief.

"Yes, ma'am," Charlie replied gravely. "You hear about it all the time. Just watch the news on any given day and most likely there will be a report of a Christian being killed somewhere, and it's only going to get worse."

"Worse? Why will it get worse? I thought stuff like that didn't happen anymore."

"Because with every passing day it gets closer to the second coming of Christ and the devil doesn't like it. I'm not exactly sure what all the signs are, but I know that a lot have come to pass. You need to talk with Cleo; she has done in-depth studies on the end times and can explain to you if you're interested."

Amy raised both eyebrows. "I think as a Christian I need to be interested, don't you?"

Charlie started to reply when a low moan from the bed caught both of their attentions. Amy leaped up from her chair and was at Chance's side faster than Charlie could blink.

"Chance? Honey? Can you hear me?" Amy asked as Chance's eyes fluttered and tried to open.

"I'm going to go get the doctor," Charlie said then rushed from the room.

Chance moaned once more and coughed then coughed some more like he had something caught in his throat. Finally, he opened his eyes, blinking them several times as they adjusted to the light.

"Hi," he whispered roughly.

Amy wiped at the tears that fell from her eyes when she heard the voice she had been longing to hear for so long.

"Hi, yourself. Did you have a good nap?" she asked with a teasing smile.

Chance nodded then tried to sit up only to fall weakly back on his pillow with a groan.

"How long have I been out?" he asked.

"Over a month, forty-one days, to be exact. How do you feel? Charlie has gone after the doctor."

"I feel like I exploded and someone put me back together, to be honest."

Amy smiled as she nodded her head. "That's actually pretty close to right. They weren't even sure if you would ever wake up. But I have prayed and prayed and God answered my prayers!"

"You prayed? That's a new development."

"Yes, it is, but it's a good one. I will tell you all about it later," Amy answered as Dr. Reed came through the door, followed by Charlie.

"Well, it's good to see you awake, Mr. Davis. You had all of us quite concerned," Dr. Reed said with a smile as he put a stethoscope to Chance's chest to listen to his heart.

"Amy, I'm going to leave you alone. I'm so happy for you!" Charlie said as she hugged Amy tightly.

"Hang on just a second, Charlie. I want Chance to meet you," Amy said as she grabbed Charlie's wrist. "Honey, this is Charlie

Jackson. She has been my very best friend and has held me together. Charlie, this is my Chance," she said with the happiest of smiles.

"Charlie, it's nice to meet you. Thanks for being there for Amy. I know it had to be really hard on her, you know...not knowing if I would wake up or not." Chance's voice grew weaker with each word.

Dr. Reed held up a hand. "I'm afraid that Chance needs to rest. I don't even want him talking right now. I'm sure Charlie will come back tomorrow, right?"

"Oh, sure! I'm not leaving town for a few more days anyway. Chance, it was nice to finally be able to meet you. You do what Dr. Reed tells you and you will be up and at it in no time." Giving both Amy and Chance a warm smile, she left and went to look for Nate to tell him the wonderful news.

Nate saw Charlie walking toward him with a broad smile on her face and a pink flush in her cheeks. He had been visiting with Hattie while Charlie went to see Amy.

"You won't believe what happened. Chance woke up! He is talking and everything!"

"Wow! That is good news, honey. I know that Amy is so relieved," Nate said with a smile.

"I better go check on him."

"Oh, Dr. Reed is with him now," Charlie explained to Hattie.

"Like I said, I better go check on him," Hattie repeated with a wink before hurrying off.

"I'm so happy for Amy...well, Chance, too, but especially for Amy," Charlie said as she wrapped her arms around Nate's waist and squeezed.

"I know it's hardest on the ones not lying in the bed. I'm glad you could be here for her," Nate replied.

"Speaking of that, do you know who showed up in Amy's room last night? Mac!"

Nate's startled eyes flew to the angel in question who happened to be standing nearby.

Mac grinned and swept his hand down his body. "Not this Mac." In the blink of an eye he changed from a towering angel to an old man with silver hair. "This Mac," he pointed to the head of gray hair.

"Oh!" Nate replied as he saw the custodian figure that Mac had used when he was a patient. When he saw Charlie's puzzled expression at his outburst, he cleared his throat.

"I mean, oh? Really?"

Charlie nodded. "Yes, he gave her a Bible and told her it was God's diary. Isn't that a neat way of thinking about the Bible? God's diary...I love it. I would love to see Mac again. I hope we can visit with him before we leave."

Nate met Mac's eyes; Mac nodded to let him know that he would make sure that Charlie got to see her "Mac."

"I'm sure we will run across him, and I agree that is a neat way to describe the Bible, and it's very accurate. I had never thought of it like that before."

"Me neither, but now that's how I think of it, like a secret window to God's heart. Mac was very wise to use that."

Nate pulled Charlie in for a hug so she wouldn't see him roll his eyes at the angel who was taking deep bows in response to Charlie's praise.

Over the next few days Chance's condition improved steadily and he was moved from the ICU unit into a private room on another floor where he could receive visitors. Nate and Chance quickly bonded over their shared experiences. Gideon could see a lasting friendship starting to develop between the two couples.

"You know, I can't imagine what I would have done if I didn't have such awesome support from both you and Nate," Amy confided. "I would hope that every person going through something like this would be able to have such support. It truly has made a world of difference."

Chance nodded his head in agreement. "Amy is right. I know that every traumatic injury is hard, no matter how it happens or who it happens to, but with military patients it's not just the physical injuries that one has to overcome. It's internal as well," he said as he tapped the area over his heart then pointed to his head.

"My mental state was the slowest to recover, and I nearly lost something very important to me because I couldn't get past it." Nate smiled as Charlie slipped her hand into his.

"What is needed is some place especially designed to care for the wounded soldier. Both inside and out."

Nate felt Charlie squeeze his hand at Chance's words. He knew what she was thinking because the same thought crossed his mind, but they needed to discuss it in private.

Later that afternoon Gideon and the rest of the angels were all gathered in Nate and Charlie's hotel room. Nate had called the family together to tell them what was on their minds.

"I think it's a wonderful idea!" Charlotte said with a little bounce. "More importantly, I think it's something that Sherrilyn would approve of!"

Gideon agreed with Charlotte's statement although the mention of his dear friend's name made him wonder where Sherrilyn and Edgar had been of late. They hadn't popped in in quite some time. He had been so busy that he hadn't noticed. Now he felt a pang in his heart that he thought might be what missing someone felt like.

Nate paused after he had told the family about their idea. Sabrina and Devon both looked to be on board; Cleo's smile said that she was in agreement as well.

"I think Sherrilyn would love to have Lost Haven used for this! It's already a rehab facility, so all you would need is some former wounded soldiers to help," Sabrina said.

"That's something we want to talk to Chance and Amy about. Since it was his idea, I have a feeling that he would be more than willing to help out. Of course, that would also mean relocating to Mountain View, but we want to offer it to them and see what they say," Nate replied.

"I know that Amy is a Christian; what about Chance?" Devon asked.

Charlie smiled. "I don't think he is right now, but I have feeling it won't be long before he accepts Jesus. He can see such a change in Amy that he is curious."

"Will Lost Haven provide any kind of medical care? If so, then a lot of renovations will need to be made to the estate, not to mention the medical staff that will need to be hired," Devon pointed out.

Nate shook his head. "We haven't got that far yet. Charlie and I just felt God speak to our hearts when Chance said what he did, so we honestly don't know what all God has in mind just yet."

Devon smiled. "Good enough, then. We will all pray with you and be seeking God's will for what parts we will all play in this."

"I already know my part. I know they will need a good cook! I just can't imagine what they are cooking up in that place now," Cleo said with a huff.

Charlie looked at Cleo with surprise. "Why, Cleo! You can't be thinking of moving back! What will your family say?"

"And just why can't I be thinking of moving back, missy ma'am?" Cleo asked with her brows raised high.

"I... I... mean we would love to have you...but..." Charlie stammered to a halt, looking to Sabrina for help.

Sabrina laughed at her daughter's helpless expression. "I think what Charlie is trying to say is that your family got you back only a couple of years ago. Won't they be upset if you move back?"

Cleo rolled her eyes and crossed her arms in a defiant manner. "Do you know what those kids of mine had the nerve to do once I moved back? Live their lives, that's what! Why, after the first two months they got so busy doing what they do that it wouldn't matter if I was there, here or in Timbuktu! I would see them about as often. I need something to get up for every morning, and I had already decided that I was moving back even before you called me. So, what do you think of that?"

Charlie rushed over and wrapped her arms around Cleo. "I think that is wonderful. I'm so happy!"

Gideon looked over at Kavik. "Did you know about this?"

Kavik looked as surprised as the others. "Not at all! I knew she was bored, but I had no idea that moving back to the estate was on her mind," he admitted with a smile, "but I sure don't have a problem with it!"

Chance and Amy's faces were ones of stunned disbelief after Charlie and Nate had finished telling them their plans with Lost Haven.

Nate snapped his fingers and waved his hand in front of Chance's face. "Dude, are you okay?"

Chance blinked a few times then shook his head. "Not really; it's not every day that you find out your new friends are multi-millionaires. This might take a few minutes to sink in."

Nate laughed, "Yeah, I feel your pain. I felt the same way when I found out. But as you can see, they are just regular people."

Amy pointed a finger at Nate. "You do realize that you're included in that, right?"

Everyone laughed at Nate's startled reaction when it occurred to him that he was indeed included. Since marrying Charlie, he was now as well off as she was. He looked over at his wife, who was sitting next to Amy with an amused look on her face.

"We didn't sign a pre-nup or anything. Why wouldn't you want to do that?" he asked.

Charlie shrugged. "I didn't feel any need in that. My blessings are now your blessings. Do you intend to run off with the money?"

"Of course, not! You know me better than that!" Nate said indignantly.

Charlie lifted her hand in the air. "So, why are we talking about it?" She knew she made her point when he opened his mouth then shut it with a snap.

"Now, we told you all of that to ask if you would be interested in a mentoring position at Lost Haven once you are fully recovered. We realize that would mean relocating to Mountain View, North Carolina, but it's really beautiful there and we think you will love it."

Chance and Amy locked eyes for only a second before they both nodded. "We would love to!" they both said at once.

Faith's Legacy

Later that night Gideon walked the roof of the hotel. He needed some air and some open space. If he closed his eyes and listened to waves crashing onto the shore, he could almost pretend he was home listening to the waves of the Crystal Sea. Of course, a hotel rooftop in California did not smell like heaven, nor did it sound like heaven, with the sounds of traffic and voices often lifted in anger. Now discouraged with his fantasy, he sighed and opened his eyes then let out an undignified yelp as he took a couple of stumbling steps backwards.

"And hello, to you, too, big guy," Sherrilyn said with a crooked grin. Edgar snorted at the look of shock and surprise on Gideon's face.

"What's the matter -- don't they teach you to always be on guard in Angel Warrior 101?"

Resisting the urge to place a hand over his now thundering heart, Gideon smiled at his friends. "They do teach that, and, to be honest, *I* have taught that, but I guess I didn't listen very well to my own instructions. Heart attack aside, it's wonderful to see both of you!" He leaned down and gave Sherrilyn a tight hug then shook Edgar's hand.

"We just thought we would pop in and check on you. How's it going?" Sherrilyn asked.

Gideon gave her a rueful grin and a shake of his head. "It has been interesting, to say the least." Briefly he gave them a quick rundown of the events of the last few weeks. When he was done, they both looked a little shell-shocked.

"Wow...interesting is right! Disturbing would also be a good word choice. My goodness!" Sherrilyn exclaimed.

"So, what will stop Karau from finding another willing participant and starting all over again?" Edgar asked with a deep frown.

"Not a thing. He can resume his plan as soon as he finds someone else who can do what Savanna did. All it will take is time."

"Yes, but surely witches who are as smart in the area of DNA splicing and gene mutation aren't exactly on every street corner, right?" Sherrilyn pointed out.

Gideon nodded, "Probably not, but in time he will find another. What we need is to eliminate the idea all together."

"But in order to do that, you would need to permanently destroy Karau," Sherrilyn said with a confused frown. "How can you do that?"

Gideon glanced down at his wrists. "I can think of one way."

Chapter 16

Zareck paced the room as the other angels watched in stony silence. "It is forbidden!" he finally said in response to Gideon's plan.

"So is what Karau is planning. You know as well as I do he won't give up on the idea, especially now that he knows it will work," Gideon said in a tired voice. He knew that Zareck would have deep reservations about his plan; he did, too, but he was out of ideas.

"Personally, I would like to gather up every one of the evil things and toss them all in there. Would sure make our jobs a lot easier and the world a much nicer place," Shana said, crossing her arms over her chest. She still had flashbacks of Karau sliding down her blade and giving her his mocking smile. A shudder slithered up her spine at the memory.

Zareck gave her a hard look. "You know we can't do that!" he snapped.

Shana rolled her eyes as she held his stare. "I said I would *like to*, not that I was *going to.* Pay attention."

"Listen, the Creator has a plan and we all know what that plan is. There is a reason why they will all be tossed into the lake of fire at the end, but we *cannot* pre-empt his plan!" Zareck said as he paced the floor, his black wings flaring in agitation.

"Well, then what *can* we do? This idea of Karau's cannot be allowed to materialize, and he came very close to doing just that," Charlotte asked Zareck with a pointed look and rapid tapping of her bare foot.

Zareck stared up at the ceiling and expelled a long breath. "I don't know, but I know we can't do that."

"Well, all of this arguing back and forth is pointless because it wouldn't work anyway," Kavik said from his spot where he had been leaning against the wall listening.

"What do you mean?" Gideon asked.

"Karau is not the only demon who knows about DNA splicing, not anymore." Kavik pointed out, "Every demon who has seen him recently knows about it. Even if we toss Karau into a cauldron of molten iron, the idea won't be extinguished unless we toss in everyone who has seen him, and we have no way of knowing who has or hasn't."

"So, we toss them all in to be safe," Shana said with a slightly evil grin then held up her hand. "Chill, Zareck, I'm only kidding. I know we can't do that, I really do," she said when Zareck scowled at her.

"The only way to stop the plan would be to make them lose interest, and the only way that will work is if they think it doesn't work," Charlotte said as she paced the floor, slowly tapping her finger against her chin as she thought out loud. "Any ideas on how to do that?" she asked the group. But no one had a clue...

Charlie hugged Dr. Reed and Hattie tightly. As much as she was eager to get back home, she was going to miss these dear people. After promising to keep in touch, they left the hospital and headed toward the airport where her parents were waiting with Brody, Savanna and Pastor Tony. They had prayed over the situation last night and with Karau currently out of commission and the hospital now seemingly back to normal, they all felt they could return home. They made plans to pack up and leave early the following morning.

"Next time we come out here, I hope we can vacation more and do less spiritual warfare," Charlie said as she slid in beside Nate.

"I'm sorry, baby. I know as a honeymoon this was pretty bad."

Charlie laughed. "I'm really not complaining, although I'm sure it sounded like it. This was educational at best and terrifying at worst." She paused as she thought over the events of the past few weeks. "Actually, you know what? I wouldn't change a thing. Our honeymoon was full of adventure and warfare with some sweet romance thrown in along the way. We helped to save a hospital, a witch accepted Jesus, a demon was defeated and we made some really great friends. If that isn't a 5-star honeymoon, then I don't know what is!"

Nate smiled at her enthusiasm, "Romance, huh?"

Charlie nodded happily. "Yes, surely you have noticed Brody and Savanna? Methinks a wedding might be in the not-too-distant future!" she sang out.

"Wow... they are barely dating and you already got them getting married. Do you think you might be rushing things a bit?" Nate asked with a straight face, knowing Charlie was about to flip kittens on him.

Sure enough, those blue eyes of hers tossed sparks his direction as she sat sideways in her seat so she could stare at him. "Nate Jackson! It doesn't take everyone years and years to finally decide what they want! Some people have sense enough to know a good thing when they see it!"

"Hey, I knew you were a good thing way back in elementary school. I couldn't resist those curls then and I still can't." Reaching out, he pulled gently on a soft strawberry blonde curl that hung tantalizingly near Charlie's left eye. "I believe you were the one who took forever to realize how much you adored me."

Charlie smacked his hand away. "You did not know that you loved me in elementary school. You were just a child."

Nate shrugged as he navigated his way through the traffic. "Maybe I didn't know it was love, but I knew you made me feel *something*. That's why I chased you all the time. Now admit it -- I knew first."

Charlie crossed her arms over her chest and set her chin in the stubborn way he knew so well.

"Come on... say it. I was first!" Nate goaded.

"Fine, you knew first. But honestly you were so annoying! I wanted to bring Moppet to school to bite you but mama wouldn't let me!" Charlie's lips twitched as she tried to keep from laughing, but she was doomed when she looked over and saw Nate's lips twitching as well. They both burst out in laughter and Charlie knew that their relationship would never be what anyone would call normal; she wouldn't have it any other way.

Gideon and Shana exchanged smiles in the back seat. They both knew that Charlie and Nate were soulmates and that God had matched them up a long, long time ago.

The next morning, Sabrina, Devon and Cleo all chatted with Savanna and Brody until Charlie and Nate arrived. Devon looked down at his watch.

"You two were starting to worry me. Our plane leaves in less than thirty minutes. It takes forever to get through security these days."

"Sorry, it took longer to say goodbye. I can't believe how I am going to miss everyone!" Charlie said with a sad smile. "But I did get to see an old friend this morning!"

"Really? Who did you see?" Sabrina asked.

"Do you remember me telling you about Mac? The old custodian that worked at the hospital?"

Sabrina's eyes brightened. "Oh, I do remember you telling me about him. You said he was very sweet to you."

Charlie nodded. "He was more than sweet; he was a life saver. He really helped me to keep it together sometimes. I hadn't seen him since we returned, so I assumed he had retired. But then Amy said he came into Chance's room one night and spoke to her. She said he seemed to know exactly what to say. He even gave her what looked like a brand-new Bible and told her it was God's diary."

Sabrina laughed softly. "That's a new way of putting it, but I like it. So, how did you see him this morning?"

"Amy called me just as we were getting in the car to come to the airport. She said that she saw Mac and told him that I wanted to see him, so she called me and we went to the hospital for a quick visit. He really is just the sweetest thing!" Charlie gushed.

Nate thought he was he was going to be ill watching Mac preen under Charlie's lavish praise. He wished she would hush. The angel had a big enough ego as it was.

Then Charlie grew somber. "He really did pull me away from the edge a time or two. I will forever be grateful to God for placing

Mac there for me." She brushed away a tear. "I think that's his job more so than cleaning rooms. He cleans hearts."

For once Mac looked humbled and touched. He laid his hand across his heart and spoke to Charlie even though she couldn't hear him.

"It was my utmost pleasure, Charlie."

Nate inclined his head slightly in thanks to the angel who, for all his outlandish ways, truly had been a Godsend to them both.

Charlie then turned to Savanna, hugging her tightly. "Oh! I'm going to miss you!"

"I'm going to miss you, too." Savanna slipped an arm around Charlie's waist. "I told Brody we will have to come out for a visit real soon."

"Yes, you do! You and I have bonded. Being tossed into a trunk together will do that," Charlie teased as she hugged the pretty redhead.

"No joke, although if you don't mind, maybe we can find a new hobby?"

Charlie laughed then pointed a finger at Savanna, "Hey, as long as we are not summoning demons, I'm game."

Savanna lifted both hands into the air. "I'm done with that mess. I promise! I'm on a new team now."

Pastor Tony stepped up next to Savanna, "Not to worry, Charlie. I will keep a close eye on our girl here and make sure she stays out of trouble."

Brody took Savanna's arm and pulled her out from under Pastor Tony's arm and placed her snuggly under his.

"No offence, Pastor dude, but if anyone is keeping a close eye on this beautiful lady, it will be me!" Everyone laughed and Charlie gave Nate a knowing look.

Cleo stepped up and took Savanna's hand. "Missy ma'am, I need you to understand something. Just because you are finished with the devil don't mean he is finished with you. No, ma'am! He will come after you now more than ever to see if you will stick to your guns. Don't you give him not nary an inch because he will take a country mile. Do you understand my meaning?" Cleo asked with a stern expression.

"Yes, ma'am. I understand exactly what you're saying. I will keep my guard up. I promise," Savanna vowed.

Cleo smiled and hugged her warmly then whispered something that only Savanna could hear before stepping away.

Devon clapped his hands then reached down for the suitcases at his feet. "Okay, we better make our way inside. I want you to know that there will always be a place for you in our home and you have a standing invitation to come anytime. In fact, I insist on it!"

"Oh, yes, you have to come and see our place and Lost Haven!" Charlie said with a wide smile.

"I'm sure a visit will be planned very soon. You folks take care, but before you go, let us pray over you." Everyone gathered in a circle and joined hands as Pastor Tony prayed for God's protection over his new friends.

Faith's Legacy

Gideon sighed in relief when the truck rolled to a stop at Devon's and Sabrina's. The two-story log home was a sight for sore eyes and he was sure glad to see it. As beautiful as California was, he had grown quite partial to the green of North Carolina, although the colors of fall were now starting to show.

Luke and D.J. came hurrying down the steps to hug their family and help with the luggage. Their blue eyes so much like Devon's lit up when they spotted Cleo getting out of the back seat.

"Cleo! We didn't know you were coming!" they said in unison as they both tried to hug her at the same time.

"Boys! Let her get out of the truck, for goodness sake," Sabrina scolded gently, but Cleo wasn't complaining. She let the twin terrors, as Charlie had dubbed them long ago, wrap her up in hugs and kisses.

"Oh, my boys! Look how you have grown!" She stepped back and eyed them both closely. "Why you're nearly as tall as your daddy!"

D.J. puffed out his chest. "Yup! Mama said she thinks we might be even taller one day!"

"How have you been Cleo? How's your family?" Luke, the ever thoughtful one, asked as he picked up her suitcase.

"Oh, they're fine, just fine! Just busy as a hive of bees; that's why I decided to move back here, where hopefully I am needed!"

"Oh, you're needed all right!" D.J. said with a loud whoop of joy! "Can we have some Cajun Boil tonight, Cleo? Can we?"

Devon stepped in and attempted to corral his son's enthusiasm. "I think we will be eating take-out tonight, son. We are all tired and jetlagged. Let Cleo get settled in; then I'm sure she will try to fill your bottomless pits."

Charlie smiled and shook her head at her brothers' antics as both of them circled Cleo like excited pups. After asking Nate to take their bags up to her old bedroom, Charlie walked across the yard to the pasture gate, slipped two fingers into her mouth, let out a piercing whistle, then listened. Within seconds she could hear the unmistakable sound of pounding hooves headed her way. Across the pasture, she could see the flying mane of her beloved Stormy as he raced toward her with his tail held high like a banner fanned out behind him. Quickly going through the gate, she waited until he slid to a stop in front of her and shoved his nose hard against her chest, knocking her back a couple of steps. Charlie giggled as she wrapped her arms around his neck and buried her face in his mane. Feeling the prickle of tears, she inhaled his warm scent.

"I have missed you so much!" she whispered as Stormy turned his head to sniff and snuffle against the back of her neck. Laughing with pure joy, she grabbed a handful of mane and tossed her leg astride his broad back and with no more than a nudge of her knee, she had him spinning around and flying back across the pasture.

Nate leaned against the porch railing and watched as horse and rider quickly disappeared from sight. Devon came out and patted him on the back.

"Better get used to that. Those two have a bond unlike anything I have ever seen."

"Oh, you don't have to tell me that," Nate replied with a shake of his head. "I wouldn't dare try to come between those two. I know I would lose," he laughed.

Devon cocked his head and gave Nate's statement some thought before he smiled and nodded. "Without a doubt!"

Charlie smiled as she felt the power of her horse beneath her as his long legs flew across the ground. The wind his speed generated whipped her hair back from her face. By simply leaning left or right, she could tell him the direction she wanted to go, and the horse responded quickly and smoothly, obeying her demands as they moved as one across the open fields. This was her happy place; this was where she could completely blank out her mind and just be. It was almost as if she could absorb some of Stormy's energy and feel it surge through her veins like a drug. This was her addiction!

Finally, she pulled back on his mane and shifted her weight backwards, telling him to stop. Stormy slowed then came to a walk before stopping all together, his sides heaving and his nostrils flared from their hard run. Slipping from his back, she shook out her legs, feeling the strain of unused muscles in her inner thighs.

Faith's Legacy

"Whew, I'm already out of shape!" she said as she walked in circles in front of her and Nate's old fort. She picked up some limbs that had fallen on the top and tossed them into a pile before she dropped to her knees and crawled inside. Flopping over on her back, she stared up at the pine branches that they had woven together to make the roof. She knew that they would soon build a home nearby, but she would try to keep their fort intact for as long as she could. Perhaps one day their children would play inside its branch walls. The thought of children brought a small smile to her face as she laid her palm on her flat tummy. Perhaps even now a new life was growing inside her. She knew that Nate would be a great father to their children and she hoped they had a houseful! But she knew that was all in God's hands. For now, she was content with it being just the two of them. They had plenty of time for babies.

The thought of time brought Lost Haven to her mind and she knew that was something she wanted to get started on right away. In fact, perhaps they should live there until they got their house built. It would make sense, she reasoned. Although the log cabin had enough room for them, living at the estate would give them both more a sense of being independent, and she knew how important that was to Nate. Anxious to discuss her idea with her husband, she crawled out of the fort and mounted Stormy, turning him toward home.

Skye and Raphael listened in amazement as Gideon and the others took turns telling them what all had happened in California. Having been recently upgraded from Guardian Angel to more of a Warrior Angel, after Luke made the decision to become a missionary, Raphael whipped out his sword and jabbed the air.

"Man! I wish we could have been there! I need to practice my demon slaying!"

Zareck laughed as he watched the blonde angel dance around, stabbing his sword at invisible foes.

"Calm down. You will get your chance, I assure you. I wouldn't go wishing for trouble."

"In truth, little brother, trouble will come sooner than you expect and usually from a direction you don't anticipate," Kavik said as he stepped forward suddenly, and with a practiced flip of his wrist he had Raphael's sword flying through the air.

"Hey! No fair! I wasn't ready!" Raphael complained loudly.

"A warrior must be ready at all times!" Shana said as she slipped behind him and swept his feet out from under him.

Gideon chuckled at Raphael's look of dismay at being so easily defeated. Holding out his hand, he pulled him to his feet.

"We all have need of training, Raphael. Don't let them get to you. We will get you whipped into shape before Luke leaves to parts unknown. He isn't even seventeen yet; we have time."

They all spent the next few hours working with Raphael and Skye, showing them moves and counter attacks until both angels were much improved. Gideon had every confidence that Raphael would make a great warrior, for he took his role very seriously. Luke would be well-protected wherever the Creator decided to send him.

That night at the dinner table Charlie brought up her idea of moving into the estate until their house was built. To her surprise her mother seemed against it at first.

"Why would you want to do that? We have plenty of room right here," she protested.

Devon reached over and placed his hands over hers. "Honey, they want their own space, and goodness knows there is plenty of that at Lost Haven."

Sabrina saw the look in her daughter's eyes begging her to understand, so she nodded her head. "Oh, I see. It makes sense to be nearby during the renovations, I suppose. I had just assumed that you would live here, is all." Then smiling bravely, she added, "We should all go over first thing in the morning and check things out. Cleo, that will give you a chance to check out the kitchens and everyone can pick out their rooms." With plans made to get up early and head to Lost Haven, everyone said goodnight and headed up to bed.

Chapter 17

The family pulled up to the estate bright and early the next morning. Nate shook his head as he took in the sheer size of Lost Haven.

"Somehow, I always forget how huge this place is," he said as he got out of the truck. Charlie grinned at his awed expression.

"Yeah, it was an awesome place to live. I remember racing my tricycle up and down its endless hallways and don't even get me started on playing hide and go seek!"

Nate chuckled, "I can imagine. I think I'm going to need a GPS to find my way around."

"I was tempted to drop breadcrumbs myself," Sabrina chimed in, "but you will learn your way around quicker than you think. I based all my directions starting from the kitchen. That was one room I could always find." She tapped her nose with one finger. "I just followed my nose!"

"Yeah, and now that you're lucky enough to have Cleo cooking for you, there will be all kinds of awesome smells to guide you," D.J. said with a grin. "Hey! Maybe I can move in, too!" His hopeful expression quickly fell when Devon shook his head.

"Not a chance, buddy. I still need you at home where I can annoy you properly!" he said as he reached out and locked his arms around D.J. in a wrestling move that had them both scuffling for dominance. While Devon could still overpower his son, he knew it wouldn't be much longer that the tables would turn. Even now he had to rely on his skill and experience more than strength.

Sabrina walked up beside Cleo, who was looking at the rose bushes that had been Edgar's pride and joy, with a sad smile. She could guess what her dear friend was thinking, for she was thinking it, too.

"It won't feel right without Edgar, will it, Cleo?" Sabrina asked softly.

Cleo shook her head, "No, ma'am, it surely won't, but that's all right, because I have his memory right here in my heart, and that will have to be good enough!"

Faith's Legacy

Gideon smiled as his eyes drifted over the familiar stones and catwalks of the estate that still held mysteries he had yet to unravel. He was happy that he might have the opportunity to explore its hidden nooks and crannies once more. He couldn't wait until he saw Edgar again. He knew his friend would be most happy to find they were once more taking up residence within the estate's walls.

Amaris, the head administrator, came down the steps with a bright smile. Charlie and Sabrina had called her earlier and told her of their plans. She had been fully supportive and looked forward to their visit.

"Good morning!" she called out cheerfully. "I hope you don't mind but I told a few key people about your plans and everyone is really excited to help you get started." The woman's gray eyes sparkled with youth and vitality despite her being in her mid-sixties. She ran circles around most of the younger staff and always seemed to be in constant motion. She chatted with Sabrina and Devon as they walked inside, telling them about some thoughts she had about the upcoming project. Cleo let them talk business as she hurried on into the kitchen. It was just like she remembered it: Spacious with seemingly miles of granite counterspace for working and professional-grade appliances throughout. The oak cabinets gleamed from a recent polishing and the red tile floors were exactly how she remembered them. She couldn't help but remember how Edgar had guarded the kitchen as his domain and how she knew she was finally accepted when he allowed her access to it.

"Well, you old coot, I hope you are enjoying your time up in glory, and I hope you know how much you are missed down here."

A tall man with a thin dark goatee and a tall chef's hat walked into the kitchen, giving Cleo an assessing look with narrowed hazel eyes.

"Can I help you?" he asked in a high-pitched voice that had a very distinct French accent.

"Hello, my name is Cleo and I will be helping in the kitchen," she explained with a bright smile.

"I do not understand. I hire all the new help and I do not recall hiring you. So, there must be some mistake," he said with a severe frown.

"Oh, I am friends with the owners. I used to work for them and now I have returned. I'm not taking anyone's position or anything. I'm just here to help out where I can."

Crossing thin arms over an equally thin body, the man peered down his nose at Cleo. "As I have already stated, there must be a mistake, for we have no need for any help in this kitchen. I will show the way out."

Feeling a prickle of temper, Cleo jammed a fist on one hip. "Now you listen here…"

"Oh, I see that you have met our head chef! This is François. He graduated head of his class in France. We are very fortunate to have him," Amaris exclaimed as they all entered the kitchen. François tilted his head in a regal manner, shooting Cleo a knowing glance.

"Yes, I was just telling François that I would be helping in the kitchen, but I don't think he was made aware of my coming," Cleo said with only a tinge of irritation in her voice. If there was one thing that got her hackles up, it was snooty people, and the head chef seemed to be the snootiest of the snooty!

Amaris tilted her head as she studied the situation for a moment. "Oh, perhaps I did forget to mention you to him. I apologize. But it doesn't matter -- I will tell him now. François, this is Miss Cleo, and she will be helping you in the kitchen. I will leave it up to the both of you to sort out the details." Turning to Charlie and Nate, she introduced the family to the chef as well.

"This is Sabrina and Devon Lane and Nate and Charlie Jackson. Nate and Charlie will be living here as well as Miss Cleo. They have wonderful plans for Lost Haven and will begin renovations soon."

François bowed in greeting. "It will be my utmost pleasure to work for you. I will make sure that only the very best is prepared in this kitchen for such a fine family."

It was all Cleo could do not to roll her eyes over the classic suck-up move that François had just made. Taking a deep breath, she silently prayed for patience. After all, Jesus died for snooty François, too!

Gideon snorted at the look on Cleo's face. He knew without her saying that she was praying for patience. Kavik rubbed hard at his face to try and erase the grin that was threatening to erupt.

"Oh, my... I don't know if putting Miss Cleo in the same kitchen with François is a good idea or not!" Charlotte said with a look of dismay on her pretty face.

"I think it's an excellent idea myself," quipped Mac.

"For who? You or them?" Charlotte asked.

"Me, definitely, me!" he replied with a grin. "This is going to be epic."

Over the next few weeks Nate and Charlie, along with Miss Cleo, settled into their new home. As Sabrina predicted, Nate learned his way around much quicker than he had thought. Before long he was navigating the estate's many hallways and rooms with ease. Charlie, too, reacquainted herself with the home that she lived in until she was five. Memories came flooding back as she spotted different things that reminded her of her childhood. They had also gotten permission from the bank to start with the renovations. They wanted to add a small wing for patients who still needed some medical attention. While they wouldn't be able to receive the same care that they would at a major hospital, they wanted to be able to treat the ones who were on their way to recovery and needed only follow-up care. The next step was finding the medical staff.

Charlie huffed out a breath as she tossed yet another resumé on the ever-growing pile. "I have no idea what I'm even looking for!" she exclaimed.

Nate smiled. "I know what you mean. They all seem highly qualified, but I want more than a qualified doctor or nurse...I want them to have a certain quality..."

"Christian...we want them to be Christians with the love of Jesus in their hearts," Charlie said.

"Exactly. I think we need to stop and pray. This was all God's plan from the beginning and we need to be careful not to take over," Nate said as he, too, tossed another resumé back on the pile. Reaching for Charlie's hand, he and she bowed their heads and prayed that the one who created heaven and earth would bring the people he wanted here to create a place of peace and healing in Lost Haven.

"Assez! What are you doing?"

Cleo nearly jumped out of her skin at the shouted command coming from François as he stood in the doorway of the kitchen with his hands on narrow hips and a horrified expression on his face.

Putting the piping bag down on the counter, she wiped her hands on a nearby dish towel.

"I am putting the filling in the deviled eggs. What in the world does it look like I'm doing?" she asked as he lifted the bowl and sniffed it with a disgusted look.

"This is horrible -- throw it out!" he demanded.

Cleo's eyebrows rose in the air. "I most certainly will not! There ain't nothing wrong with that filling! I make the best deviled eggs in four counties back home."

François tilted his head so he could peer down at her. "Clearly, they are lacking in taste if *that* is what's considered to be the best," he said, putting air quotes around the word *best*.

Cleo sighed as she tried to think of a way to reach some sort of understanding with the Frenchman. "Now, look. Just because I might make mine different from you don't mean mine ain't as good." She lifted the piping bag and placed a small amount of the egg filling on a spoon. "Here, try you a bite; then you can say if it's any good or not."

François recoiled like she had offered him poop on a spoon. "I will not insult my sensitive palette with such garbage!"

Popping the spoon in her mouth, Cleo chewed slowly and methodically, making yummy sounds the entire time. François spun around and walked out, muttering in French under his breath.

"Well, bless my soul! At least I figured out how to get rid of him," she chuckled then picked up the piping bag and got back to filling her eggs.

Nate handed the clipboard back to the delivery driver who was bringing in the first load of lumber for the new medical wing. Turning back to go inside, he caught a familiar figure stepping out of a cab. Hurrying over, he opened his arms to welcome her.

"Hattie! What a wonderful surprise! What are you doing here?" he asked as he hugged her tightly.

"Well, let me tell you, it's not exactly out of my own free will, but I am obedient to God and he said to come here and help you, so that's what I'm doing!" she said with a tired but satisfied smile.

"Oh, well, you are certainly needed, and you are most welcome here! I can't wait to see Charlie's expression when she sees you!"

"Charlie knew I was coming. I called her a couple of nights ago. I guess she didn't tell you?" Hattie asked with a puzzled look.

"I wanted to surprise my husband," Charlie said as she walked to them. "I knew nothing would make him happier than to have his favorite nurse on staff here. Surprise!"

Nate laughed as he hugged Charlie. "You were right! It is an awesome surprise and the answer to our prayers for sure! We didn't know what we were going to do."

Hattie picked up her bags. "Well, just show me to my room and I will get to work!"

Nate reached over and took her bags. "I think tomorrow will be soon enough to put you to work. Today let's just show you around."

The next day by noon Hattie had already lined up several interviews for the nursing staff. She had also made a phone call to California and spoken to Dr. Reed for possible recommendations for a full-time doctor. Promising to give it some thought, he said they would hear from him by the weekend. Watching Hattie bustle around ordering the medical supplies and speaking to the contractors about making sure each room had enough electrical outlets and what kind, Charlie sent up a prayer of thanks to God for always providing what and sometimes *whom* they needed.

Charlie thought if they stayed on schedule they could be ready to receive their first guests in the new wing by early spring. Pulling her phone out of her back pocket, she was shocked to see the date. It was already nearing the end of October and they hadn't even brought out their fall decorations! Taking off across the house, she grabbed Nate and Hattie then headed out back to the shed.

"I lost all track of time," she said as she stuck the key in the massive door. "We need to get out our fall decorations. There is giant Tom Turkey that is my favorite in here somewhere!" Jumping right in, Charlie hurried up and down the aisle looking for the correct season.

"Found it!" she called out. Turning around, she saw Nate still standing at the door with Hattie, who looked utterly gob smacked.

"What. On. *Earth*?" Hattie said in disbelief as her eyes took in the towering shelves of the warehouse-like building that were packed with every conceivable holiday decoration.

"I know...it boggles the mind, doesn't it?" Nate said with a grin.

Hattie nodded slowly as she ventured inside. "Boggles...yes, yes, it does."

"The original owners of the house had a slight obsession with holiday decorating, from what I have been told."

"Honey, I like to decorate, but this borders on madness!" Hattie exclaimed.

Laughing at the nurse's facial expressions, Charlie leaned against the wall only to fall right through it when it slid open.

Chapter 18

Shana gasped in surprised as Gideon threw himself on the ground so Charlie would land on him instead of the piles of broken mortar and steel rods that littered the ground. He was positive that this tunnel had not been in the diagrams that he and Edgar had pored over. The fact that it appeared to be unfinished told him that perhaps his old friend didn't even know about it.

"Charlie! Are you okay?" Nate called out as he knelt to help her up. Brushing his hands over her arms, he spun her around, looking for any sign of injury.

"No, I'm fine; it just startled me." Looking around, she pulled out her phone once more and flipped on the flashlight app. "Gosh! Look at this place? What do you suppose it was used for?"

"It looks like they never finished whatever their plans were," Hattie said as she poked her head inside. Their voices echoed eerily through the dark tunnel that went further than the light from the cell phone would shine.

Taking a few steps further into the tunnel, Nate exclaimed, "Hey! Look at this -- There are stacks of Bibles back here!"

Hattie and Charlie carefully made their way to where Nate was standing. Shining her light, she could see old crates with the word AMMO stamped in red on the sides. But instead of ammunition they were full of wrapped Bibles.

"These look old…really old," Charlie said as she picked up a Bible and felt how brittle with age the paper was that covered it.

"Are they just regular Bibles?" Hattie asked.

Nate nodded. "It looks like it. Standard King James. Why would they have so many and were they going to ship them somewhere or were they shipped here?"

"And why are they stamped AMMO, but have Bibles inside?" Hattie threw in.

Charlie shook her head. "I don't know, but I remember hearing Mama talk about how Edgar and the previous owners were all tied in to the Holocaust. I think Edgar was put into a camp. I need to talk to her and see what she remembers him telling her. This might have something to do with that."

"I bet it does. The Bibles look old enough to be from that time, but let's come back when we have more light and after we talk to your folks," Nate suggested.

Gideon wished he could find a way to reach out to Edgar. He might or might not have any answers for the many questions that he had, but his friend was the only one he knew to ask.

Later that night Charlie and Nate were seated at Sabrina's table eating dinner and telling the family about the secret tunnel. Charlie was somewhat surprised at her mother's less-than-surprised reaction.

"That old place is full of secret tunnels and passageways. I know where some of them are, but I'm not surprised that you found another one."

"Did you ever find one with crates marked AMMO, but that actually held Bibles?" Nate asked.

"Oh! No, but I found a secret room inside one once. It was full of old pictures of the Lasker's and Adolf Hitler. That's when we finally started getting some information out of Edgar about the house and his previous employers."

Sabrina told the story about how Edgar had come to be with the Lasker's, since Nate and the twins had never heard it. When she finished, the table was silent as everyone thought about the horrors that poor Edgar and the others had gone through.

"So, Mr. Lasker was a doctor?" Charlie asked.

Devon nodded. "Yes, although I believe he was a medical scientist as well. He invented new medicines that were very powerful and very disgusting." He recalled with a shudder the memory of swallowing the foul-tasting liquid.

Sabrina cracked up at the expression on Devon's face. She remembered all too well the night he had shown up beaten black and blue with broken ribs and lacerations. At the time, she had no idea just what he was involved in, although if she was being honest, that was when she realized that she had much deeper feelings for him than she had been admitting to. It wasn't until later that she learned that Devon was a bounty hunter and spent his time looking for criminals who had jumped bail or were otherwise wanted by the authorities. Although he no longer did that job, and hadn't for many years, he still carried that quality of always being watchful and aware of his surroundings. Sabrina always felt safe when she was with her husband. She knew whatever came their way, Devon was more than capable of dealing with it.

"Do you suppose that the Lasker's were shipping the Bibles back into Germany? Perhaps that was why the boxes were marked AMMO." Everyone stopped eating and considered Luke's words.

"I think that's most likely exactly what they were doing. Good thinking, son," Devon said with a wink. "Edgar said they were very much against the regime, although they had to give every appearance of supporting it. Dr. Lasker was even involved in treating Hitler."

"Treating him for what?" Charlie asked.

Devon shrugged, "I don't know exactly, but the magic formula that Lasker had invented was for him. So, clearly he was sick with something."

"I don't understand how one human being could harbor so much hate for his fellow man," Nate said with a shake of his head.

"Well, you have to understand that Hitler did not work alone. He was heavily influenced if not totally under control by the enemy. That's the only explanation for such evil," Devon replied.

"You're talking about the devil, aren't you?" D.J. asked.

"Yes, son, I am. You need to never forget that he is out there. After everything we experienced in California, I'm certain more than ever that he knows his time is ending. He will become bolder and try to influence more and more people."

"But don't people want to do bad stuff anyway? I mean, without the devil's help?"

"Oh, sure they do. Man, can come up with all kinds of awful things without any influence of evil, but the bad ones, like Hitler and others, I believe were influenced. I really don't understand how anyone can have such hatred in their hearts for another human being without being influenced in some way. It really doesn't make any sense, if you think about it," Devon replied.

Faith's Legacy

Gideon knew for a fact that as much as people loved to use the old expression "the devil made me do it," there were a lot of bad things done that the devil didn't have any part of. Mankind can be creators of evil all by themselves. They hated and in turn taught their children to hate. It was an ugly, vicious cycle. But he agreed with Devon about Hitler -- That kind of hatred was spawned from the pits of hell. The world would grow increasingly fuller of hate as the time for Christ's second coming drew closer.

Savanna sat next to Brody in Pastor Tony's church trying to pay attention to the sermon, but she had been feeling ill all morning. The throbbing in her head had gotten so bad that she now felt nauseous. Brody gave her a concerned look, but she smiled up at him and shook her head to tell him she was fine. But she wasn't...not by a long shot. If she didn't know better she would swear someone was driving a stake through her skull! When Pastor Tony finally closed the service with a word of prayer, Savanna had never been so relieved. All she wanted to do was go home to her new apartment and lie down for the next twenty years or so. As they got up from the pew and slowly made their way to the front door, she felt a tug on her sleeve. Turning around, she saw a small elderly woman smile up at her.
"Excuse me, dear, but do you know you have a demon poking his claws into your head?" the woman said with the sweetest of expressions.
Savanna knew her eyes must have bugged out of her head at the woman's words. Unable to form a coherent sentence, she reached out and grabbed Brody by his shirt to pull him to a stop. When he turned around, he saw her pale face.
"Honey, what's wrong?"
Savanna just pointed to the woman standing behind her still smiling as if she didn't just blow Savanna's mind with her outrageous statement. Not understanding what was happening, Brody asked the woman if they could help her.
"Oh, no, I'm not the one needing help; she is," she replied, pointing at Savanna. "I just told her that she had a nasty old demon poking his talons into her head."

Savanna would have burst out laughing at the expression on Brody's face except she was sure she had the same one still on hers. Brody's eyes immediately went to the top of Savanna's head, but he didn't see anything. When he turned back to the woman, she shook her head.

"Oh, I know you can't see him. I wish I couldn't, but, trust me, he is there. Tell me, dear, does your head hurt?"

Savanna couldn't keep the tears of pain from her eyes as she nodded her head yes. Brody looked at her with a frown.

"Why didn't you say something? We could have prayed for you," he admonished gently.

Savanna shrugged as she squinted up at him, the pain increasing with every passing second. "I just thought it was a headache. It wasn't until right before the service ended that I thought it might be something more, although I didn't think a demon was doing it."

The woman patted Savanna's arm. "Don't worry, my dear. I will get rid of it." Reaching into her purse, she pulled out a small bottle of anointing oil and dabbed a little on Savanna's forehead. Savanna pulled back, looking around at all the people.

"Wait! You're just going to do it right here? In front of everyone?"

The woman peered at her through narrowed eyes. "Now which concerns you more? People's reactions or getting rid of it?"

"Getting rid of it!" Savanna answered without hesitation. At this point she didn't care who saw or what they thought. The pain was unbearable.

Placing her hands on either side of Savanna's head, the woman started praying. She spoke quietly but with such power that her hands grew warm against Savanna's scalp. Within seconds the pain vanished as if it had never been.

"Oh! It's gone! Thank you so much!" Savanna reached out and hugged the woman, "My name is Savanna Becker."

"Pleased to meet you, Savanna. That's a lovely name! I'm Odilia May Walker, but everyone calls me Odie, and I have been coming here since before Pastor Tony could see over the pulpit." She beamed up at Brody who was still looking somewhat confused. "I know it can be hard to understand, son. Would you like to come to my house for lunch? We can talk about it and perhaps I can help you understand it a little bit better."

"I wouldn't want to intrude…" Brody started to say before Odie waved her hand at him.

"Don't be ridiculous! I rattle around in that old house all by myself most days. It will be pleasant to hear someone else's voice besides my own." She gave them both a wink. "The conversation will be more entertaining, too! I will just ride with you. Most of the time I walk to church; it's good for the old thumper!" Odie said, giving her heart a solid thump with her fist.

So, within an hour Savanna and Brody found themselves seated at Odie's lace- covered dining table enjoying a pot of beef stew and cornbread. Once they had all eaten their fill, she invited them into her "parlor." It was a very feminine room filled with floral print furniture, little tables covered with ceramic figurines and lacy doilies draped across the back of every chair. Brody carefully perched on the edge of a delicate-looking wingback chair. He was sure it would collapse under his weight.

"Now, I'm sure you have questions," Odie said with a serene smile as she clasped her hands demurely in her lap. She looked every inch of the lady that she was, definitely not your typical demon slayer, although, to be truthful, neither Savanna or Brody was sure what that looked like.

"Do you actually see the demons?" Brody asked first.

Odie tilted her head to one side as she pondered his question, "Not exactly. At least I don't see them in the way you think. It's like I get an impression, a swirl of negative energy that forms a picture in my mind. I can generally make out what they are doing without being able to see them clearly. Does that make sense? It can be difficult to explain." She tilted her head once more then chuckled, making her blue eyes twinkle. "Although I do believe this is the first time I've tried. So, how did I do?" she asked.

Savanna smiled at Brody then at Odie. "You did fine. I think I understand how you see them, and I guess my question now would be why do you see them?"

Faith's Legacy

"Now that, I don't have an answer for. I have always been able to sense things, not dead people or future events or such as that, but just energy. Every living creature gives off energy, some good and some not so good. In time, I learned how to 'see' it and how to get rid of the nasty stuff." She gave Savanna a very direct look.

"I'm not certain what you have been dabbling in, my dear, but I have my suspicions that it isn't anything good. Am I correct?"

Savanna looked everywhere but into Odie's all-seeing gaze. "Yes, ma'am, I was a practicing witch, but I gave all that up," she was quick to point out.

Odie nodded her head. "I see. You may have given 'all that' up," she said, "but I don't believe it has given you up. Don't think they are going to go away just because you don't want to play with them anymore. Once you have opened that door, it is far harder to close it again."

Savanna leaned forward in her chair, beautiful green eyes begging Odie for her help. "Can you help me close it again?"

Odie shook her head. "That's not my door to close, but I can tell you how to do it. The only thing that will defeat the darkness is light. You must surround yourself with God's light, both inside and out."

"How do I do that?"

"First, you read God's holy Word, every chance you get! Fill your heart and spirit up with scripture. Then you make sure that the people you spend time with are good, solid Christians. You cannot associate with anyone from your past who is still living that lifestyle. Next, play praise and worship music in your home, in your car, on your phone. Saturate the very air you breathe with praise to our God. Oh! I should have said this first: Throw out anything and everything that had anything to do with witchcraft, no matter how small or insignificant. Throw it out and burn it! Don't leave anything for the darkness to latch on to. By doing all of this, you will create an atmosphere that will repel evil and firmly shut the door." Odie paused and gave Savanna a stern look. "Once you have done all of this, the devil will still come against you, but once you have firmly established that you're done with him and there is no longer any room for him in your life, you will be able to stand against him. But for now, you need to heal and to grow strong in the Lord."

Brody, who had been pretty quiet during the conversation, leaned forward in his chair. "I think we need to go to North Carolina."

Savanna nodded in agreement. "My thoughts exactly!"

"What is in North Carolina?" Odie asked with an interested smile.

"We have good friends there. I can't think of stronger Christians to be with right now than Nate and Charlie Jackson and their family."

Odie nodded. "Sounds perfect!"

Across the country, Charlie fell facedown across her bed in total exhaustion. The new medical wing for Lost Haven was coming along but she never would have guessed so many decisions needed to be made on a daily basis.

"I'm still just a kid, or at least I feel like one right now," she mumbled into the bedspread. Feeling her muscles slowly start to relax, her eyes drifted shut only to spring back open when the cell phone in her back pocket vibrated. Groaning, she pulled it out and answered it, thinking it was probably another question she needed to answer.

"Hello?" she sighed.

"Charlie? Is this Charlie? This is Savanna Becker." The voice on the other end sounded unsure.

"Savanna! Hi! How are you? It's great to hear your voice!" Charlie sat up on the side of the bed, feeling new energy rush over her at the sound of her friend's voice.

Savanna laughed. "Hi! I'm good! I was just wondering if there was room in that giant house for a couple more people?"

"There is enough room in this house for a couple dozen more people! Are you and Brody coming for a visit?"

"Yes. I need to get away from here, and North Carolina sounded perfect. We can be there by the end of the week, if that's okay?"

"Of course, it's okay! I can't wait to see you! Is everything alright? You sound tired," Charlie commented.

"I'm fine. You sound tired yourself; are *you* all right?" Savanna replied with a chuckle.

Charlie groaned slightly. "You would not believe how much is going on right now! We are about halfway done with the new medical wing, plus we have found new tunnels that we have no clue what they are for."

"Tunnels? In your house?"

"Oh, I'm sorry. I forgot that you have never been here and don't know the history of Lost Haven. It's too long to go into over the phone, but I will tell you all about it when you get here. You need two rooms, right?"

Savanna smiled as she looked down at the small diamond on her left hand. "Yes, please." She couldn't wait to tell her friend the happy news: Brody had proposed to her last night. He was so sweet and so nervous that he dropped the ring three different times trying to slip it on her finger. Savanna finally had to do it herself after she had said yes, of course. She knew that Brody Miller was her forever love. It didn't really matter that they had only recently reconnected. Never had she felt so safe and in sync with another person. She had heard people use the expression "soul mate," but she didn't really believe in it until now. Brody was truly her soul mate, the one chosen by God to walk with her on this earth until he called them home. They hadn't set a date yet, but she knew it would be soon. After finalizing her plans with Charlie, she hung up the phone and picked up the Bible that Pastor Tony had given her. Flipping it open, she ran her hand across the smooth pages that had been highlighted and underlined by his late wife. It was easy to get to know the woman by reading what scriptures had touched her heart. Savanna decided that it wouldn't be the worst thing she would ever do to follow right in her footsteps.

Chapter 19

Gideon stood with Shana, Charlotte, Zareck, Kavik and Mac as the construction workers started putting up the walls for the new wing. Watching everyone's breath frost the air, he was glad that he couldn't feel the cold bite of the winter air. November had been unusually cold, at least according to what the weather man had said this morning on TV. Charlie was so wrapped up all you could see was her blonde ponytail and her eyes peeking out from under her knit hat and scarf. Sabrina danced from one foot to the other trying to stay warm as the men talked about the progress and what they could do to make it easier for the workers. They had already brought in portable heaters and kept coffee and hot chocolate readily available for them, but they still looked miserable. Nate wanted to tell them to go home, but they had all decided they wanted to reach a certain point before they stopped for the Thanksgiving break. Most of the workers were good guys, but Gideon was keeping a close eye on one in particular. He had several demons slithering in and out of his body. So far, he hadn't done anything other than what tasks were given to him, but he made Gideon's wings twitchy. One thing he had learned over the course of his lifetime was never to ignore a twitchy wing.

Charlotte clapped her hands in excitement. "Oh, I can't wait for the new medical wing to open up! Just think of all the new hearts that will receive Jesus!"

Kavik nodded. "Yes, little sister, this is a good thing, a very good thing. The warriors need a place to recoup and to heal from not only the physical damage to their bodies, but also the mental and spiritual damage. I know that Sherrilyn will be so pleased."

That night Gideon paced his old familiar path along the roof line of Lost Haven. He had spent many nights up here when Charlie was young. It seemed impossible that she was now a grown woman. How quickly the years had passed. They must seem to pass even faster for humans who were only allotted a certain amount of time on earth. He felt the air stir next to him, and Sherrilyn, along with Edgar, appeared.

Faith's Legacy

"Hi, there, big guy!" Sherrilyn's smile was just what he needed as she reached up for a hug. He had never been a hugger prior to meeting this wonderful person, but now he found he needed hugs.

"Hello! It's great to see you!" he said as he hugged her, being careful not to squeeze her too tightly. Turning to Edgar, he grasped his hand.

"I see you're back to your old habit of pacing the roofline. At least now you don't keep me awake at night!" Edgar teased with a smile.

Gideon snorted. "Old man, nothing kept you awake at night, least of all my pacing two stories above your head."

"What has you worried tonight?" Sherrilyn asked.

Stepping back a few paces, Gideon shook his head and lifted his hands. "Honestly? I'm not sure. I feel extremely uneasy." Lifting his eyes, he studied the clear night sky. "There is a storm coming. If I can figure out from which direction, maybe we can be ready for it."

"I know you will figure it out and be ready for it," Sherrilyn said as she patted his shoulder reassuringly.

"How do you know that?" he questioned.

Sherrilyn shrugged. "Because you always are." Then she smiled and pointed to the new construction that was underway. "I love what they are doing with Lost Haven, by the way! This is becoming so much more than I had ever dreamed or envisioned." Walking over to the edge of the roof, she looked down at the work site.

"This is your legacy, your Faith's Legacy," Edgar said to Sherrilyn with a proud smile. "What you have started, another will finish."

"Oh! That's beautiful, Edgar! Yes, this is my legacy. I wish people could understand that we will see the fruits of our faith, if not on earth, then in heaven. The Lord is so sweet to let us see that what we started will be completed."

"They met some wonderful people in California who are going to help," Gideon added.

Sherrilyn nodded. "Yes, Amy and Chance Davis. They will be great! I'm so glad that they both have given their hearts to Jesus."

Gideon raised his brows in surprise. "I knew that Amy had, but I didn't know about Chance. That is wonderful news!"

"Yes, he did it just last night. All of heaven is rejoicing, as with every salvation." Sherrilyn's smile grew even bigger.

The three friends enjoyed each other's company for the rest of the night and by the time they left, Gideon felt much more like his old self.

A few days later a yellow cab pulled up with two heads hanging out of the passenger windows in the back. Savanna and Brody stared in stunned disbelief when they arrived at Lost Haven.

"I know they said it was big, but this place goes way beyond big!" Savanna said as she tried to get her jaw to close.

"You speak the truth, my little foxy lady. I think they downplayed it just a bit," Brody said as he got their bags from the trunk. After tipping the driver, they hurried up the circular steps and rang the doorbell. After a few seconds the massive door opened and they saw Cleo's smiling face.

"Why, Miss Savanna! Mr. Brody! Come on in! It's colder than Satan's heart out here!"

Savanna and Brody chuckled at Cleo's colorful description of the weather, not that they didn't agree with it. It was cold, especially to people who were used to the balmy weather of California. Once they were inside, they both craned their necks, looking up at the skylights that were in the entry-way. Cleo simply smiled and waited while they looked their fill. She remembered well the first time she had stood in this spot and it was something that needed a moment to take in!

"Wow!" Savanna said in a hushed whisper.

"Yes, it is breathtaking, isn't it?" Cleo replied. "They don't make grand old estates like this anymore."

"Duuuude...I don't know if they ever made houses like this! This place is incredible!" Brody said as he took in the gleaming hardwood floors that stretched out in front of them. Cleo gave them the grand tour, showing them the dens with the massive fireplaces that all had blazing fires, the mantles tastefully decorated with fall leaves and flowers. They both oohed and aahed when they entered the sunroom that was bright and surprisingly warm with the south-facing glass walls and ceiling that let in the sunlight. Lush plants lined the benches that circled the walls. Holding the place of honor in the center of the room was a water fountain with a nine-foot-tall maiden pouring water out of a large urn. Savanna walked over and looked into the bottom of the fountain and wasn't the least bit surprised to see colorful tropical fish swimming in its depths. She turned to Brody with a delighted grin.

"That's it -- I'm never leaving!"

"I hope you never do!" Charlie stood in the doorway watching her friends' awed expressions. Walking quickly toward them, she held out her arms in welcome.

"Welcome to Lost Haven! I'm so happy to see you!" She hugged them both then stepped back and gave them a delighted smile. It took her only seconds to notice the sparkling diamond on Savanna's left hand.

"Ooooh! Let me see! Let me see!" she squealed as she lunged for Savanna's hand.

Savanna laughed as she held out her hand so Charlie could admire the ring.

"This is wonderful! I'm so happy for you! You didn't say a word when you called!"

"I know. I wanted it to be a surprise!"

"Well, it was! And a very good one, too. Nate is around here somewhere. Let's go see if we can find him. I know he will be as happy to see you two as I am."

As they passed the kitchen, they heard a loud crash. When they looked inside, they saw François standing in the middle of the kitchen with a pile of shattered china scattered at his feet. He looked at Charlie with a bewildered expression on his face.

"François! What happened? Are you okay?" Charlie asked as she stepped carefully over the shattered remains of what once was a very nice china collection.

"*Oui*, Madame, but I do not know what happened! One moment I was walking across the kitchen and the next plates were tumbling from the shelves. They seem to have flung themselves across the room!" The chef's normally pale face was even more void of color as he tried to explain what he had seen.

Cleo joined them a few seconds later with a look of dismay on her face.

"Why, land's sake! What on earth happened?" she said as she looked at the pile of broken china.

The chef's pointed nose rose a few inches. "As I was telling Madame, I was walking across the kitchen when all of the china fell from the shelves. Perhaps you did not stack them properly after dinner last night?" There was no mistaking the accusation in his voice.

Planting a fist on her hips, Cleo lifted her finger. "Now I believe I know how to lay one plate on top of another!"

"Clearly, you do not," François said with a slight lift of his nose.

"Hold on, everyone!" Charlie said, trying to head off what was most likely going to be a heated argument.

"François, you just said that the plates seemed to fling themselves across the room; that's not falling because of not being stacked properly. See, if they had simply fallen off the shelves, they would be on the floor below the shelves. They are a good six feet away in the middle of the floor," Charlie pointed out.

"Yes, well…" François huffed as he crossed his arms. "Even so, that must be the reason. China does not toss itself across a room," he insisted.

Charlie shrugged. "Maybe not, but that's what you said it did and the evidence to back up your story is right there at your feet. You know as well as I do that Cleo had nothing to do with this."

The chef sniffed slightly. "Perhaps not," he finally conceded.

Cleo rolled her eyes as she went to the closet and got out the broom and the dust pan. "That old snoot blames me for everything. If his quiche falls, it's because I walked too close to the oven. If his gravy has lumps, it's because I was using his favorite whisk at the time. Honestly, he makes sure to imply that everything is my fault," she muttered as she knelt to pick up the pieces of china.

"Cleo, I'm sure that François feels very bad for insinuating that this was your fault, don't you, François?" Charlie asked, giving the chef a direct look.

Once more the chef sniffed in distain. "Perhaps. It is possible that I was in error."

Cleo dumped the broken pieces into the trash bin. "Perhaps? Perhaps you need a lesson on how to apologize!" She raised her hand when Charlie opened her mouth, "Now, I am well aware that wasn't a nice Christian response, but what you got to realize is I ain't perfect yet. I know that the good Lord is using this old corn cob to smooth some of my edges." Cleo eyed the chef with narrow eyes. "I think I just figured that out right now. So, François, you just keep on with your rubbin' and one day I will look like a shiny new diamond!" With that said, Cleo turned and walked out, humming softly under her breath.

"Did she...did she...I do believe she called me an old corn cob!"

Charlie, Savanna and Brody all doubled over in laughter at the look on the chef's face.

"Yeah, bro, she did...but if it helps any, you're lucky she didn't call you something worse!" Brody said with a chuckle.

"But why would she call me such a thing? I do not understand." François asked in a bewildered voice.

Charlie took pity on the man and explained what Cleo had meant. "You know that Cleo and most of us here at Lost Haven are Christians. We believe sometimes Jesus will use other people to teach us things about ourselves that we need to work on. I suspect that with Cleo it's patience."

"Why did she tell me to rub her? I refuse to give her a massage! I will turn in my resignation at once if that is to be expected of me!" he exclaimed hotly.

Charlie shook her head as she waved her hands. "No, no... it's a figure of speech. To rub someone the wrong way. That means that you and Cleo don't get along too well because you're so different, or perhaps too much alike. It kinda works both ways. But it will all work out. Don't worry about it and keep on with whatever you were doing. I will make sure that we order new plates to replace the ones that were broken."

Faith's Legacy

As if he had forgotten, François looked once more toward the open shelving that held the plates. He shook his head then went on about his work.

Charlie led her guests upstairs to show them their rooms. She gave Savanna the room that she and her mother had shared when they first came to Lost Haven and placed Brody down the hall. That night they all finally got together with Nate and discussed their happy news. Nate's smile grew wider when he heard they were engaged.

"I'm so happy for both of you! Now Brody, don't be the idiot I was and let her get away! You get her last name changed ASAP!"

"I remember how beautiful Mama and Devon's wedding was. They had it here in the fall," Charlie said with a dreamy smile. Then her eyes popped open as an idea hit her. "Hey! Why can't you get married here? We can make it so beautiful for you and of course we won't charge you a penny!"

Nate gave her a patient smile as he placed his hand over hers. "Babe, they may have their own ideas about where they want to get married. Besides, you have to remember that this was only a home when your mom got married. Now it's a rehab, and having a wedding might interfere with something they have planned."

Charlie nodded as her face turned pink. "You're right, I'm sorry. I just get carried away sometimes."

"It's okay, Charlie. We honestly haven't even thought of where or when the wedding will be. But we really appreciate your offer," Savanna said with a smile.

"What about Thanksgiving? Can you stay for that or do you have plans?" she asked with a hopeful look.

Savanna looked at Brody who shrugged. "I don't have any plans, so if you're free, I wouldn't mind staying."

When Savanna smiled at Charlie, Charlie threw up her fist in the air. "Woo-hoo! This is our first Thanksgiving here as a couple, so we are happy you will be joining us." Then her face crinkled in thought.

"What's the matter?" Nate asked.

Savanna and Charlie both looked at one another and spoke at the same time…

"François!"

Chapter 20

The man moved slowly and methodically through the work site, careful to keep in the shadows. The last thing he wanted was to get caught now when he was so close to completing his assignment. Carefully stacking some scraps of lumber into a pile, he pulled out a small bottle of lighter fluid and squirted it on the pile. Once he was satisfied that he had enough of the flammable liquid on the lumber to do the job, he struck a match and tossed it. For a few brief seconds the flare from the explosion of flames illuminated his face and his black eyes.

Gideon stood staring out of the bedroom window while Charlie and Nate slept. He could hear Shana and Mac chatting in the background but he had tuned them out as he looked out onto the dark landscape. He was so lost in thought that it took him a few seconds to register that the orange glow he saw wasn't supposed to be there.

"Mac! Something is on fire down at the new wing! Wake up Nate. I'm going to go see what is going on! Shana, go get Kavik!"

In a flurry of activity all three angels jumped into action. Mac reached out and shook Nate's shoulder.

Nate grumbled as someone shook his shoulder, pulling him from sleep. Thinking it was Charlie being playful, he rolled over to capture her hands only to find her fast asleep.

"Nate! It's me! Something is on fire at the construction site!" Mac's voice propelled Nate out of bed. Hopping over to the window on one leg, he looked out and saw the ominous orange glow.

"Here, let me help you." Mac had grabbed his prosthesis then stood next to him so he could put a hand on his shoulder to balance while he slipped it on. Nate turned and woke up Charlie.

"Charlie! I need you to call 911. There is something on fire at the construction site." When Charlie opened her eyes, Nate repeated his instructions.

"On fire? How on earth did something catch on fire?" Charlie questioned as she hurried across the room for her cell phone.

"I have no idea, but I'm going down there after I wake up Brody and a few others." A knock on the bedroom door had them both looking at each other. When Nate opened the door, Brody and Savanna were already standing there with two of the residents. Mitch and Bradly, he thought were their names. He knew Mitch was there as a recovering meth addict; he couldn't remember what Bradly was there for.

"Dude, I guess you already know something is on fire, right? Savanna already called 911."

"Oh good! I was just about to do that!" Charlie said.

"Something woke me up and I saw the glow from the flames. I called 911 then I woke up Brody. We met these two gentlemen on the way to your room," Savanna explained.

"Miss Charlie, our room is right next to the construction site so we heard the whoosh sound it made when it flared up, and I gotta tell ya from what I could see from my window, I don't think this was no accident," Mitch said with a frown.

"What did you see?" Nate asked.

"We saw that it was a pile of lumber that was burning. That pile wasn't there a couple of hours ago, and no way did it catch on fire without some help. Someone started it."

"Charlie, Savanna, you two stay here with Mitch and Bradly and wait for the firemen to arrive. Brody, let's see if we can save anything."

"Nate, I'm a volunteer fireman or at least I was...I can help if you want," Mitch offered.

"That's great! Yes, we can certainly use you. Bradly, do you mind staying with the women? With all that's going on, I don't want to leave them alone."

Bradly shook his head. "I don't mind at all."

Gideon arrived at the construction site with Kavik and Shana mere seconds behind him. The pile of lumber stacked in the middle of the concrete pad was a clear giveaway that it had been set on purpose.

Kavik looked around. "This makes no sense. The fire will eventually burn itself out and not damage anything else. What was the point?"

"I don't see anything else that has been tampered with, do you?" Shana asked.

They soon heard the scream of the fire engine as it came up the road, and then Nate, Brody and Mitch all arrived. Brody started to take a long pole to scatter out the debris to slow the burning, but Mitch stopped him. "No, let it burn and don't touch it. The fire Marshall can tell more about it if it's left alone. Besides, it isn't going to hurt anything. Look, its placed directly in the middle of the concrete. Even if no one spotted it, all it would have done is burn itself out."

"Why would someone want to burn some scrap lumber? That doesn't make any sense," Nate said with a frown.

Shana raised her eyebrows when Nate asked the same question she did. Gideon had a very uneasy feeling about all of this. That feeling intensified when he felt Charlie was in danger.

Charlie wasn't sure if being annoyed was the correct emotion under the circumstances, but it was what she felt when she saw the pistol that Bradly now pointed at her and Savanna.

"Ladies, I need you to come with me, please. Just do as I say and no one will get hurt." Bradly shooed them in the direction he wanted them to go with the barrel of the gun.

"Okay, that's it! I'm taking some Judo lessons, maybe some Karate lessons, too, and any other self-defense Kung-Foo classes I can find. I'm getting a dog, too. A big German Shepard because this is seriously starting to become a problem," Charlie grumbled under her breath as they walked down the back staircase.

"Sign me up, too," Savanna whispered.

"Both of you shut up! Just walk; don't talk!" Bradly ordered from behind them.

They made their way down into the kitchen and as Charlie put her hand on the door to go outside she heard a loud THAWACK! Spinning around, she saw Bradly hit the floor without so much as a peep coming out of him. Standing behind him was Cleo brandishing a cast iron skillet.

Gideon, Mac, Shana and Kavik skidded to a stop just short of where Cleo stood holding her skillet high in the air in triumph.

"Take that, you old bad man!" she said with a wide grin.

"Cleo! Oh, my gosh! That was awesome!" Charlie exclaimed as she high-fived her friend. "How did you know?"

"I'm a light sleeper and I heard everyone up moving around so I decided to get up and see what was going on. As I stepped out of my bedroom, I overheard what he," she pointed at Bradly with the skillet, "said. I figured he would try to take you out through the kitchen door, so I grabbed my trusty old cast iron skillet and we handled it!" she said, giving the skillet an affectionate pat. Cleo glanced down once more at the man still sprawled on floor. "Mercy! I ain't done killed him, have I?"

Savanna reached out and prodded his ribs with her toe. When he moaned, they all heaved a sigh of relief.

"He is alive but I don't want him getting up off that floor. We better tie him up while we have the chance." Looking around the kitchen, Savanna spotted some aprons hanging on a hook. "There! We can use the tie strings on those aprons!" Within seconds they had him trussed up like a Thanksgiving turkey.

Gideon chuckled as he shook his head. "Well, I feel rather useless, don't you?" he asked Kavik, who gave him a rueful grin.

"That's not the first time she has used a good piece of cast iron, and I doubt it will be the last!"

"Oh! This is great! I love that woman! I really do!" Mac chortled with laughter as he held his sides.

"Looks like the ladies handled this one just fine, all on their own!" Shana chipped in with a wide grin.

A few minutes later Nate stood and stared in confusion. He looked to Brody and then Mitch, but they had the same lost and bewildered expression he was sure he had. Bradly was tied up with what appeared to be aprons while Charlie, Savanna and Cleo were all standing there looking extremely pleased with themselves.

"Hi, honey!" Charlie greeted him with a big grin.

"Hello to you, so... what's going on? Why is Bradly tied up?" Nate questioned. All three women started speaking at once, so

Nate held out his hand. "Hold on! I can't understand all three of you at one time. He turned to Cleo, who was still holding the skillet. "Cleo, let me hear your side of the story first; I have feeling it's going to be most interesting." Cleo told her side of what happened and then Charlie told hers. Nate and Brody both stared in anger at the man who was just now starting to wake up. With a less than gentle jerk, Nate got him up off the floor and set him in a kitchen chair.

Bradly moaned as he tried to focus his eyes on the very angry man in front of him. "I am going to ask you some questions, and so help me if I think you're lying to me, I'm going to let Cleo whack you with her skillet again. Do you understand?"

Bradly rolled his eyes up at Nate. He seemed to be having trouble focusing. His gaze rolled around seemingly trying to find something he could look at.

"Did you set the fire to cause a distraction?" Nate asked.

"He may have had it set, but he was in the room with me when it started," Mitch said as he paced the kitchen. "I'm so sorry, Nate. I wish I could tell you more about this guy but he just moved in a few days ago."

"Do you know anything about him? Why is he here?"

Mitch shook his head. "He said something about needing a place where he could get his head screwed back on straight. I didn't ask what his damage was, though, you know? I figured he would tell me in his own time if he ever wanted to. He was quiet, though. I mean *real* quiet. That's what I meant about him being weird. I haven't ever been around someone who can go hours and hours without talking to someone who is in the same room with you. Well, except for my ex-wife, that is."

Brody leaned down and whispered in Nate's ear, making him study Mitch carefully. The man immediately knew what Nate was thinking.

"Hey! I have been here since well before you guys moved in. You can ask Amaris if you want. I swear I didn't have anything to do with any of this."

"Well, it's clear he was following someone's orders. We need to find out who." Brody said.

"Could it be Karau?" Charlie asked.

"I don't know. I don't know how long it takes them to reassemble themselves, so to speak," Savanna answered, "but I can just about promise if it's not Karau, it's another demon."

"Do you think they are still after you?" Charlie asked Savanna.

"Maybe. I have a feeling they will always be after me to some degree."

"Who is Karau and why is someone after you?" Mitch asked with a confused look."

Everyone turned and looked at the man they had all forgotten wasn't in on any of the previous events.

"Oh, boy... this ought to be an interesting explanation," Mac commented warily.

"Karau is someone that we had trouble with earlier in California. He was very unhappy when Savanna stopped helping him with something that she no longer agreed with." Cleo's answer satisfied Mitch and told no secrets.

Brody turned to Mitch, "Why don't we wait outside for the fire department?" he gave Nate a long look as he opened the door and walked outside with Mitch, giving them the privacy they needed to question Bradly.

As soon as the door closed behind Brody, Nate started asking Bradly questions: "Who sent you? You are you working for?"

Bradly shook his head as he squinted up at Nate, "Dude, I wouldn't tell you if I knew. Whatever you threaten me with is nothing compared to what he will do to me if I talk."

Every question Nate asked was answered with non-answers. Finally, Gideon had enough. He positioned himself to the left of Nate and slipped his sword out, laying the edge against Bradly's shoulder. The man screamed as the holy light started to blister his skin.

"Stop! Stop! That burns!" he cried out, his eyes wide with pain.

Nate looked at the others. "I'm not doing anything," he said.

"Nate, you are getting a little *special* help... go with it," Mac told him with a wink.

Nate nodded to show he understood. "Bradly, you know you are taking orders from the dark side. Well, guess what? We happen to have help from the light side. The side of good and the side that will win in the end. I highly suggest you answer my questions."

Savanna and Charlie looked at Cleo to see if she understood what was going on. They guessed by the little smile on her lips that she did. Charlie scooted closer.

"What's happening?"

"We are getting a little help from our angels," Cleo replied.

Charlie's eyes grew wide. "From angels? Really? How do you know?"

Cleo shushed her, "Because I do...just watch."

"Who is giving you your orders?" Nate asked as he crossed his arms casually across his chest. Once more the man refused to answer and once more Gideon laid the flat of his sword against his shoulder, causing him to writhe in pain.

Nate shrugged, "Hey, I got all night and I can play hardball as long as you can. But I'm not the one in pain."

"Okay! Okay! Make it stop and I will tell you what I know! I swear!" Bradly pleaded.

Gideon lifted his sword from Bradly's shoulder. The sword wasn't actually burning the man, but it probably felt like it.

"This guy came to me about two weeks ago, and offered me ten grand if I started causing some trouble around here. Just petty stuff, really, nothing that would hurt anyone."

"You call sticking a gun in my wife's face and trying to kidnap her petty?" Nate's dark brown eyes flashed with anger as he grabbed Bradly up by his collar.

"At first it was petty stuff, man! At first! I know I scared the woman and I'm really sorry."

Charlie stomped over to stand in front of Bradly then stuck her finger in his face. "First off, I wasn't scared. I was ticked off -- you need to know the difference. Secondly, all you did was reinforce my plans of taking every Kung-Fu self-defense class I can, getting a huge dog, a German Shepard named Brutus, and getting my permit-to-carry license so the *next* time someone gets orders to kidnap me, they had better bring a freaking *ARMY!*"

By the time, Charlie had finished her speech, she was standing so far over Bradly he had tipped the chair he was sitting in back on two legs trying to get away from her.

The wail of the fire engine pulling into the drive stopped any further questioning. Within minutes the estate was swarming with firemen who quickly doused the flames then started asking questions. Once Nate had explained what Bradly had tried to do, they turned the investigation over to the police, who escorted him to the back of a patrol car in handcuffs.

After it was all over and the sun had started to break over the horizon, François came into the kitchen. He stopped at the kitchen entry-way, looking at everyone with a surprised look.

"*Qu'est-ce que c'est?*" he asked. When everyone looked at him with blank expressions, he repeated his question in English. "What is this? Why are all of you awake so early and in my kitchen?"

Cleo got up from the table where she had been sipping on a hot cup of coffee, "No, sir. I'm not ready for you yet. I will see ya'll in an hour or so. I need more coffee and more Jesus before I have to deal with Frenchie here. I'm sure you can explain everything that happened without me." She left the room, leaving behind a befuddled François.

Chapter 21

Over the next few days everything seemed to settle down around the estate. The repairs were made from the damage the fire had caused. As far as anyone knew, Bradly still hadn't told whom he was taking orders from, so everyone was on high alert. Charlie had kept her promise about taking self-defense classes. Both she and Savanna had enrolled in a mixed martial arts class. Gideon couldn't help but chuckle at Charlie's serious expression as she practiced her defense maneuvers; she would make a fierce warrior! She was all business and seemed to be a natural. It wasn't long at all before she was able to knock her opponent to the ground and escape his grasp. Adam, the instructor, had high praise for both Charlie and Savanna.

"Another month or two and I wouldn't want to mess with either of you ladies!" he boasted after class one night.

Savanna smiled as she wiped the sweat from her face with a towel. "That's great, but I will need to continue my lessons in California. I'm sure Brody is getting anxious to return. He is probably having 'Surfers withdrawals.'"

"Oh, has he said that? I hate the thought of you guys leaving!" Charlie said with a look of dismay.

"It's okay, babe. I can give you your lessons back in Cali," Brody said as he walked up behind Savanna and wrapped his arms snuggly around her slim waist.

Nate smiled at Charlie as he took note of her bright cheeks from her exertions. Adam walked up to the men and offered his hand.

"Hello, I'm Adam. You must be Nate. Charlie talks about you all the time."

Nate took the man's hand. "Hi, Yes, that's me. I hope she was only telling how charming I am," he said with a chuckle.

Adam laughed as he held up his hand. "It was all good, man. I promise." Adam's gaze dropped to Nate's leg. "I don't mean to be in your business, but I noticed that you walk with a prosthesis. Can I ask what kind?"

Faith's Legacy

Nate frowned slightly at the man's keen observation. He worked hard at making his stride as natural as possible and very few noticed his slight limp. But Adam seemed genuine in his questioning, so Nate lifted the leg of his jeans.

"It's just a typical transtibial prosthesis," Nate answered.

Adam nodded. "You walk extremely well with it. I had to watch closely to even notice it." He then surprised them all by lifting the right leg of his Karetegi and exposing his own artificial leg.

They all looked at Adam in shock. "Wow! I had no idea that you wore a prosthesis! You move so naturally with it!" Charlie exclaimed.

Adam smiled, "Well, it took lots of years of practice and creating the right leg." He slipped off his shoe, exposing the oddly shaped foot on the prosthesis. "See here where the foot is actually a little longer, and then here where there is a break in the arch? It's held together with tension bands. That gives me more range of motion and it moves more like a natural foot." He reached down and unstrapped the leg then handed it to Nate as he stood perfectly balanced on his left foot, "Here, it's a right leg and our heights are close enough that this should fit you pretty good. Try it out and you will see what I mean."

Nate hesitated for a moment as he looked at the others who were still in training class.

"Don't worry about them. They are doing their own thing. Trust me, you want to try this. It will blow your mind," Adam said with an encouraging smile.

Nate took the leg then walked over to a nearby chair and quickly changed it out with the prosthesis he had. Standing up, he noticed the difference before he ever took a step. By the time, he had walked across the room, he was smiling.

"Dude! This is fantastic! It really is almost like my natural stride. Where do I get one?" he said with a huge grin as he walked back to where Adam was still standing on one leg. He quickly swapped them out again and returned it to Adam.

"You can get it right here. I created it. That is my side project that I work on when I'm not teaching martial arts."

"Do you mind if I ask how you lost it; was it in the war?" Nate asked, noticing the Marine Corp tattoo on Adam's forearm.

"No, it wasn't in the war. I actually escaped that relatively unscathed. It was a motorcycle accident. A semi failed to stop at a stop sign and literally ran me over, crushing my leg beyond repair. It's been nearly eight years ago, now."

"What you have created is incredible. Are you trying to market them? I know you would have an overwhelming demand for them."

Adam shook his head. "No, I've only recently come up with my workable prototype. I've made a few here and there for people, but I haven't seriously considered going into business fulltime. Believe it or not, I don't exactly make a bank teaching self-defense classes, and the start-up cost alone would be more than I could afford."

"What about arm or hand prostheses? Do you have plans or ideas for those, too?" Nate asked.

"Actually, I do," Adam replied. "You see, a leg prosthesis is fairly basic, but an arm and especially a hand prosthesis are a lot more complex because of all the fine motor skills that you use. I know you can get the ones that have computer chips in them that read the muscle movements in your arms and can interpret the movement that you want; however, those are insanely expensive, and most can't afford them. I think I can make one, using the same tension band idea. It would grip and hold most everyday items such as a drink or even a hammer, enabling someone who worked with his hands for a living to be able to go back to work to some capacity." Adam grinned when he realized how long he had been talking. "Sorry, as you can tell, I'm kind of passionate about this."

"Yeah, that's kind of hard to miss. It's cool, though. This world needs more people who are passionate about their work," Nate said with a laugh as he held out his hand. "Tell you what, keep what I said about going into business on your mind. I need to talk with the boss here," he looked down at Charlie, "but I want to talk to you some more about this."

Faith's Legacy

Adam's eyes lit up with surprise as he took Nate's hand. "That's not a hard request to fill. I think about it all the time anyway. I hope to hear from you soon."

That night Charlie crawled in bed and reached over to gently rub the deep frown lines between Nate's eyes. "You sure are thinking hard about something. It's Adam, isn't it?"

Nate smiled as he folded his hand around Charlie's. Bringing her fingertips to his lips, he kissed them softly. "Yeah, I really think he needs to sell what he has created. There is a real need for a low cost and a better functioning prosthesis."

Charlie tried to stifle a yawn as she snuggled under the covers. "So, help him. You know we can afford it."

Nate glanced down at her. "You see that's part of the problem. I need something productive to do with my time. I need to earn my own way."

"And you don't feel like you do that now?" Charlie questioned with a puzzled frown. "You work all the time, especially with the building of the new wing," she pointed out.

"All I do is receive deliveries and write a check. I need more, Charlie. I need something that I can contribute to. I could seriously get involved in this thing with Adam. I might not be able to develop the product, but I can promote it and help him market it. I can even help test out some of it. Soon we will most likely have customers right here at Lost Haven that could benefit from it." He rolled over until he was propped up over Charlie. "Tell me you understand."

"Are you bored?"

Nate sighed then rolled over onto his back. "No, Charlie. I'm not bored. I don't want to be a 'kept' man. My whole reason for reenlisting in the first place was so I could earn my own way. I know we have money, but it's your money. I have always been one to make my own way. I need this. I need to feel productive and useful and..." Nate trailed to stop when Charlie kissed him gently.

"I get it, Nate. I do. I was only teasing when I asked if you were bored. Mama said that Devon had the same problem when they got married. That was why he worked so hard for so many years. You do what you need to do. I love you and I want you to be happy."

Nate returned her kiss with a happy smile. "Thanks, babe. You're the best!"

Charlie laughed, "Well, yeah, and don't you forget it!"

The next day the estate was strangely quiet. With all the residents gone for Thanksgiving, silence echoed everywhere *except* the kitchen. That room currently resembled a battlefield as Cleo and François squared off over the Thanksgiving meal that was to be served the following day. Cleo wanted the traditional meal of turkey and dressing, with the typical side dishes of green bean casserole, candied yams, mashed potatoes, broccoli salad and yeast rolls, while François had prepared a much more sophisticated menu.

"Why am I even here if I cannot showcase my culinary talents at such a revered American holiday?" he complained loudly with his arms propped on his narrow hips.

"I think you just hit the nail on the head, American holiday," Cleo muttered under her breath.

"What was that?" François demanded.

"I said that being it is an American holiday, maybe an American ought to fix it! Land's sake, I don't even know what most of the stuff on your menu is, and where is the turkey?"

"It is a fine well-orchestrated symphony for the palette. I have created a glorious blend of colors and textures that will be a delight to all the senses, without that crass barnyard animal on my table!" François replied with a huff.

Cleo stared at him blankly for several long seconds. "Colors and textures? For heaven's sake, are we going to eat it or paint with it?" Finally, she sighed after sending up a hasty prayer for patience. "Look, why don't we fix both? We will have more than enough people here to eat it all and truly, I would hate to deprive anyone of your well-orchestrated delight or whatever you called it, but I want something on this table people will actually know what to do with."

"Prepare both?" François replied with a frown.

Faith's Legacy

"Yes, I believe they call that compromising. Don't you do that in France?"

"Fine," he replied with a sniff. "Let us prepare both and you shall see that when it's offered, people prefer finer foods."

Cleo waved the dishtowel she was holding over her head like a flag of surrender. "Fine, let's just get something cookin'; we're running out of time."

The two cooks spent the next few hours prepping for the massive meal. Cleo placed her giant twenty-five-pound turkey in her special brine to soak overnight. After that she started baking several pans of cornbread for her dressing. As she worked, she couldn't help but glance over at François's work-station to see what he was preparing, but she couldn't make heads or tails out of the pile of ingredients he was working with. It was too bad they couldn't seem to get along. She would love to learn some of the different recipes. Struck by sudden inspiration, or maybe it was conviction of the Holy Spirit, she would decide which later, she walked over to where François was chopping up vegetables like a mad man.

"You know, I always wanted to go to cooking school. I love to cook and would love to learn some of your skills. Do you think you could show me some tricks and techniques sometime?"

She watched as several different expressions crossed the man's face, before he finally nodded without looking at her. "*Oui*, I will show you a few simple techniques after the holiday."

Cleo turned away before he could see her smile...

The next morning everyone in the estate woke up to the most wonderful smells coming from the kitchen. Both Cleo and François had gotten up long before daylight to start preparing the meal. When Charlie and Nate walked into the kitchen, they both stopped in surprise. Instead of the epic battle of kitchen, which they expected, they found Cleo closely watching François as he slowly whipped thick cream into high, frothy peaks.

Charlie lifted her eyes to Nate, who was watching with the same surprised expression she wore.

"Wow... a Thanksgiving miracle!" she whispered.

Nate slowly nodded, "No other explanation."

"If you two are finished whispering over there, how about you come give us a hand?" Cleo fussed without ever taking her eyes from François's hands.

Hours later the large table was filled with so many incredible dishes that the family stared in awe and amazement.

"Heaven, this is what heaven smells like, I'm sure of it!" D.J. said as he sniffed deeply. Lifting a cover from the dish nearest to him, he tried to pinch off a small bite but was thwarted by Sabrina's stern look from across the table.

"Charlie, the table looks just beautiful!" Sabrina praised.

Charlie smiled happily as she gazed at all the faces that sat around her table. This was the first time her entire family had been together since her wedding, and her heart was filled with such happiness and... well, appropriately enough, thanksgiving. Everyone joined hands and bowed their heads as Evan gave thanks for the meal.

"Dear Heavenly Father, we come to you today with hearts full of thanksgiving for all of your many blessings. We thank you for seeing us safely through another year. Lord, we thank you for all the new faces that have joined our family, and we ask that you continue to lead us and guide us, in Jesus's name we pray, amen."

D.J. waited until he got the go-ahead from his mother before he dove for the nearest dish. Luke chuckled as he watched his brother attack the meal like it had offended him.

"So, Luke, have you decided where your first missionary trip will be?" Carl asked as he started filling his plate.

Luke shook his head. "I haven't decided on anything for sure, Grandpa. But I do have a few places that are top on my list."

"You can't really go anywhere until you graduate, can you?" Catherine asked with a concerned look. "You're still too young."

"Actually, I can go now. I would just have to go during school breaks and during the summer. I'm old enough to go as long as I have signed permission from my parents and an adult willing to go with me," Luke replied, nodding his head toward his parents.

Gideon noticed that Sabrina kept her gaze on her plate and didn't respond to the conversation. He knew that letting Luke go was going to be extremely hard for her. Sabrina liked her children to be where she could keep an eye on them. Charlie's trips to California during Nate's recovery and during their honeymoon were hard enough. Luke being off in places unknown was going to be torture for the over-protective mother.

"Are you planning on going somewhere this summer?"

Luke nodded as he avoided his mother's gaze. "I would like to go to Cuba. They have recently opened up the borders and now would be an excellent time to bring the news of Christ."

"Cuba!" Sabrina said, her blue eyes wide with shock. She turned worried eyes to Devon. "Oh, surely not, honey. That place is still very unsettled. Why don't you find somewhere in the U.S. to go? I know there are places here that need you." *I need you!* She screamed silently.

Devon reached over and placed his hand on top of Sabrina's. "Honey, summer is still a long time away. We have plenty of time to discuss it with Luke," he said gently.

Sabrina nodded as she drew in a deep breath to calm her nerves. Devon was right; summer was still several months away. Surely by then Luke would reconsider, or she just wouldn't sign the permission slip!

The conversation then turned to Savanna and Brody's engagement. "Have you set a date yet?" Sabrina asked.

Savanna smiled as she looked over at Brody. "No, ma'am. We were engaged right before we left to come up here, so we really haven't discussed it yet."

The next hour was spent enjoying the wonderful meal that Cleo and François had prepared and discussing wedding plans. Gideon noticed that Luke did more pushing his food around than eating it. He gave Raphael a nudge with his elbow.

"He is really serious about this Cuba thing, isn't he?"

Luke's guardian nodded. "Yes, he has been studying the country for weeks now. His heart is set on going."

"I really don't see Sabrina allowing that to happen," Skye said as they all looked over where Sabrina was laughing at something that D.J. had said.

"I can promise she will fight this with everything in her." This came from Charlotte. "Her mother's heart will hate the very idea of her baby leaving and going to such a dangerous place."

"True, but her heart needs to see that Luke and D.J. are not babies anymore. Luke has a very mature nature about him. He is calm and steady, and he thinks things over carefully," Kavik commented.

"Cleo's son in-law and daughter were missionaries, weren't they? Surely Cleo can help Sabrina learn to let go," Raphael said with a nod toward Cleo.

Kavik shook his head, "No, you have to understand Cleo and Sabrina raised their children in very different times, and they have very different parenting skills. Cleo was essentially a single mother. She relied on her boys going out and making a living to help her with the family. Sabrina has lived a very blessed life to be able to keep her boys at home under her wings. It will be hard for her to open up and let them fly."

Gideon looked over at Sabrina. He knew what Kavik said was very much the truth. Letting Luke go was going to be one of the hardest things Sabrina had to face, but face it she must, for even Gideon could see the calling that was on the young man's life.

After everyone had eaten, they all retired into the den where a cheerful fire was blazing in the massive fireplace. Savanna backed up to the hearth and released a deep sigh as the heat slid up her back, relaxing her muscles.

"Oh, this feels so good! Brody, I want a fireplace in our home," she said with a smile.

Brody grinned at her. "Well, sweetheart, I hate to break this to you but where we live there would be very little reason to light a fire."

Savanna's face crinkled up into such an adorable pout that it made Brody want to declare winter the national season of California. He would trade his surfboard for snow-skis. He could adapt -- if only he had the power to change the climate!

"Oh, well, I guess we will have to come here during the cold season to visit Charlie and her huge fireplaces."

"That sounds good to me! Whatever excuse you need to come back will be just fine," Charlie replied with a grin as she plopped down on the couch next to Nate.

"Cleo, that was an amazing meal," Nate complimented as he rubbed his full belly.

Cleo smiled. "I would love to take full credit, but, as you know, this house has two cooks now, and François made as much of that dinner as I did. In fact, I would say that he made the best parts."

"Whatever that dish was with the raviolis was amazing!" D.J. chimed in with a wide grin.

"I believe he called that Beef and Marjoram Ravioli."

D.J. crinkled his face in a confused frown. "Mary-Jam?"

The room exploded in laughter, causing the young man's face to turn bright red.

"No, honey child, not Mary-Jam. Marjoram…it's a spice that is like oregano," Cleo explained.

"Oh. Well, whatever you call it, I sure hope he teaches you how to cook it, 'cause, man, it was awesome!"

"You should go tell him, D.J. I'm sure François would love to know how much you enjoyed his cooking."

D.J. smiled at his mother as he jumped up from the couch to go do exactly what she had suggested.

Less than two minutes later, they all heard D.J. shout from the kitchen as sounds of dishes shattering reached the den. Jumping up, they all ran toward the kitchen then stopped and stared in disbelief.

Devon hurried over to where D.J. was crouched with his hands over his head like they teach in school during tornado drills.

Raphael was covering D.J. with his wings outstretched over the boy's body, covering him completely.

"Who did this?" Gideon asked, his voice shaking with anger that evil would dare step foot inside the estate.

Raphael shook his head. "Gideon, there were many of them, but I didn't see any that I recognized. They were laughing as they destroyed the place."

Gideon glanced over at Mac, who was the only angel without a human to guard. Mac read his face easily. "I'm on it," he said then shimmered from sight.

"Son, are you hurt?" Devon asked.

D.J. shook his head, "No, I...I... think I'm okay," He stammered, obviously shaken up by his experience.

"Can you tell us what happened?" Sabrina asked as she wrapped her arm around his waist. He had grown too tall for her to reach his shoulders.

D.J. shook his head. "I don't know. I came in here looking for François when it felt like a hurricane blew through the room. Stuff was flying everywhere through the air and it was cold. It was so cold in here!"

The kitchen truly did look like it had exploded. Dishes and food were thrown everywhere. On the floor, on the walls, even dripping down from the ceiling.

"Whoa!" Luke said as he stared in shock.

"What on earth?" Catherine said as she stepped closer to Evan.

"See? It's like a bomb went off or something!" D.J. said as he pointed out all the damage.

"Did you see anyone when you came in?" Carl asked, his face taking on a hard edge as years of previous cop training took over.

"No, Grandpa. I didn't see anyone."

Brody pulled Savanna closer to his side. "Does this remind you of anything?" he whispered in her ear.

"Yeah, it does, unfortunately," she answered softly, recognizing the handiwork.

"Didn't something like this happen the day we got here? Only not on such a large scale?"

Savanna nodded, "Yes, some dishes were thrown from the shelf. I just hoped it was a coincidence."

"I think we can rule that out, don't you?"

Faith's Legacy

Savanna pulled Nate and Charlie over to one side and briefly told them what she suspected was happening.

"He followed you here?" Charlie asked in dismay.

"It certainly looks that way. I'm so sorry, Charlie. I never thought about something like this happening. I will leave at once, so he will leave you and your family alone." Tears filled Savanna's eyes as she hugged Charlie.

"What are you going to do, child, run for the rest of your life? You have to face this devil head-on and stand up to him or he will never leave you alone." Cleo gave Savanna her no-nonsense look.

"How do I stand up to him?"

Cleo touched Savanna's chest just over her heart. "'Greater is he that is within you than he who is in the world,' 1 John 4:4. Jesus has given us authority over all demonic powers. You first have to believe it for yourself; then you have to make that nasty old devil know that you believe it!"

"But... but...I'm scared," Savanna admitted with downcast eyes.

"Honey, do I look scared? Look around you; do you see fear in their eyes? That devil has overplayed his hand by showing himself in this house! I can promise you that."

Sabrina walked up to stand next to Cleo. "Baby, we are right here with you, but Cleo is right. You have to show Karau that he doesn't have any power over you any longer."

The sound of a sharp gasp made them all turn to the doorway where François stood in total shock as he surveyed the damaged to his once-immaculate kitchen. Placing a hand over his heart, he slowly walked to the middle of the kitchen then looked up at the ceiling where seemingly every knife in the kitchen was deeply embedded. Holding up a hand, he shook his head.

"I do not even seek an explanation. I no longer care. I am turning in my resignation effective immediately!" He turned around without another word and marched back down the hallway to his quarters.

"Honey, this is probably just as well. We will talk to him after we get all of this," Devon waved his hand around the room, "straightened out."

Faith's Legacy

Sabrina slowly nodded in agreement, her face drawn and white with fear and worry. Looking at the total devastation, she glanced up at Devon. "How does this happen? What brought this here?"

Savanna stepped forward. "I brought this here, although I certainly didn't do it on purpose. I didn't think he would follow me."

Sabrina's eyes grew round with shock when she realized the *who* Savanna was talking about.

"But he has no right to come in this house! This has always been a house protected by God. He has no right!"

"Sabrina, in the natural world no, but in the supernatural world, maybe he does."

"Evan, I don't understand what you mean. You know that Sherrilyn was a godly woman," Sabrina pointed out as she looked up at Devon to see his expression. She saw no anger at the perceived slight to his sister, only a curiosity to Evan's meaning.

"Sabrina, you know I loved Sherrilyn, and I would never disrespect her memory, but she has not lived here in a very long time. Yes, you check up on the place regularly, but as far as what spiritual doors have been opened since you stopped living here is really anyone's guess."

Sabrina looked over at Evan in surprise. "I guess you're right, but this is all so new to me."

"Well, if it makes you feel any better, this is all rather new to us, too. This is stuff you see in horror flicks, not in your own kitchen," Evan replied with a rueful expression.

François came back out carrying two large suitcases. He paused long enough to hand Sabrina a piece of paper.

"This is my forwarding address; please send my last paycheck here. Thank you and *au revoir*." He walked away, and the sound of the front door slamming firmly made them all jump.

Carl and Keelie stepped up to Devon and Sabrina. "We are going to take Kinsley back to your place. We can pray and help cover you in prayer from there. We don't think this is something she needs to be a part of."

"Mama, the devil did this," Kinsley said in a matter-of-fact tone as she walked up to her mother's side.

Keelie turned to her daughter. "Why, Kinsley, why would you say that?"

"Because I saw him standing out in the field when we got here. He was just watching, but I know he did it."

Charlie felt goosebumps race across her skin at Kinsley's words. Placing a hand on the girl's shoulder, she asked her what she saw.

Kinsley shrugged. "I saw a man that wasn't a man. He was the devil."

Carl stepped up and took his daughter's hand. "Don't be afraid, sweetie."

A bright smile broke across the young girl's face. "Oh, I'm not scared, Daddy! I have my angel who always keeps me safe." She then leaned in and said in a loud whisper, "Don't worry, Daddy -- you have an angel, too. We all do!"

All the angels in the room looked at one another with wide eyes, except for Gideon. He had always known that Kinsley still had her spirit eyes. He wasn't sure if it was the fact that the girl had Downs Syndrome that had kept her spirit eye open, or if it was simply the way she was created, but she had always been able to see him, so he figured she could see the others, too. Although, to be honest, she seemed to understand that it was something she needed to keep to herself... until today.

Chapter 22

Gideon looked at Kinsley's guardian, Leia. The short guardian with equally short blonde curls shook her head and placed her finger across her lips, telling Gideon that whatever he wanted to say needed to be said out of earshot of Kinsley. He nodded to let her know he understood. They couldn't leave the room, so he switched to their angel language so they could speak freely without the girl understanding their words.

"Do you think she saw what she said she saw?" he asked.

Leia nodded. "Yes, I saw him as well. She looked over at me and all I could do was smile reassuringly at her to let her know that I saw him, but that she would be safe." Leia paused as she smiled slightly at the young girl. "Kinsley knows that she sees something she isn't supposed to. I have not spoken to her about it. In fact, I very rarely speak to her. Much of our communication is through looks and facial expressions."

"Does she ask questions about us?" Baylor asked.

Leia shook her head, "No, she rarely acknowledges me at all. Unless something happens like today. Then she will simply look to me for guidance and can tell by my expression what she needs to do, if anything."

"It is very unusual for a child to see the dark side," Kavik pointed out.

Skye scoffed slightly. "K-man, it's very unusual for a child of Kinsley's age to still see us, but there she stands."

The angels all looked toward Kinsley, who was watching them out of the corner of her eye. Gideon had to give the girl credit. She kept her face very natural and didn't look at all as if she were watching heavenly beings converse in their own language right next to her, but then again, she had been doing it her whole life. All of a sudden, he remembered the first time that Edgar had revealed that he could see them. Gideon had never caught on to the man's ability at all until he was ready to reveal it. Kinsley reminded him a lot of his old friend.

"It has to be this Karau you told us about," Donavan, Carl's guardian, said, his steel gray eyes narrowed in speculation.

"She said she saw a man that wasn't a man. Surely, he hasn't found someone to help him become human again so quickly," Charlotte replied.

"It would be easy enough to find someone he could possess and control. Most likely that is what has happened."

Gideon agreed with Zareck, but that didn't make him feel any better about the situation.

Charlie scrubbed hard yet very carefully on the pane of glass, trying to remove the sticky cranberry sauce that coated it. She was still trying to process what happened.

"You would think by now nothing would surprise me anymore," she muttered under her breath.

Sabrina chuckled, hearing her daughter's complaint. "The last few months have certainly been eye-opening, haven't they?"

"For sure. Honestly, I think I liked it better when my eyes were closed," she admitted with a slight grimace.

"I can certainly understand your feelings. I wish that sometimes myself."

Charlie stopped scrubbing and just stared at her mother. "You do?"

Sabrina smiled, "Of course, I do. This has all been very scary for me, too, you know."

"I guess I think of you as being brave and so sure of yourself." Charlie studied her mother closely as if seeing her with new eyes. For the first time in her life, she saw her as a woman who was still learning about things of life much like she was. Someone who didn't have all the answers or have everything figured out. Feeling suddenly much closer to her, Charlie bumped her shoulder against Sabrina's. When she looked over at her, she crossed her eyes and stuck out her tongue, causing her mother to crack up. They all spent the rest of the evening cleaning up the giant mess and being thankful that no one was hurt.

Karau paced the floor at the old feed mill. He knew it was just a matter of time before Gideon and his blasted band of merry angels swarmed the place. Turning around, he eyed the groups of

Faith's Legacy

demons that were silently watching him. *Let them come*, he thought. *I am ready for them.* They all knew who their commander was now. He glanced over at the huge vat of boiling iron ore and felt the stretching of his thin black lips. He had quickly and ruthlessly taken care of Lespar... forever.

"The very idea that that low-ranking imbecile thought he could overthrow me!" Karau's mocking laughter rang out, causing the black mass of demons to shift nervously. "Well, who else would like to try for the position? Come now, surely among you is someone who would care to challenge me." Karau strutted up and down between the rows of black-skinned, red-eyed demons, trying to provoke at least one into a challenge, but none would rise to the occasion.

"Very well, I have already fed my toy demon tonight. What it hungers for is a taste of something else...something a little sweeter and with pretty wings! I think I know of just the perfect snack!"

Mac stood at the rear of the mill watching as more and more swarms of demons filled it. He knew this was once the scene of a great battle between the light and darkness; it looked as if it would be again.

Cleo rocked back and forth in her prayer closet as fervent prayers tumbled from her lips. Things were shifting in the spirit realm; she could feel it so strongly. Feeling something touch her hand, she opened her eyes to see a piece of paper placed next to her. Gideon! He was reaching out to her, so something must be happening. Opening the paper, she read his fancy script. For a male, Gideon had some pretty handwriting.

Greetings, Cleo! Forgive my lack of communication since you have returned. I fear that the enemy is creating much havoc in the spiritual world, as I'm sure you are aware. I need you to gather the family together tonight and hold a prayer meeting. We need everyone praying with extreme faith! Pray specifically for strength in our numbers and power in our swords! Thank you for your help. I will be in contact with you at a later time.

Sincerely, Gideon

Cleo nodded as she read Gideon's note. "Yes, sir! I will do exactly what you asked. I will also call my family and have them pray for you all, too. We will have you so covered up in prayer that the enemy won't be able to get within a forty-acre field of you."

Later that evening Gideon stood before the rest of the angels on the roof of the estate to hear Mac's report of what he saw at the mill.

"There are a lot, Gideon. More demons than I have ever seen gathered in one place in a very long time," Mac said with a concerned look on his face.

"And you have no doubt that it is Karau?"

Mac nodded. "Oh, it's him. I saw him, although without his human suit it took me a minute to spot him. Apparently, there was a revolt against him and someone tried to take his place."

Gideon nodded as he tried to plan the best course of action. Mac brought him out of his thoughts by placing a hand on shoulder.

"I don't want to freak you out, but he has fired up his favorite toy. I didn't want you to be caught off guard," Mac told him quietly.

Flashbacks of scorching heat and the smell of his own flesh burning made Gideon swallow hard. Freaked out was a gross understatement to describe the cold terror that slid down his spine. He had never had anything rattle him like the very mention of the vat did. He was sure that had he been human, he would be diagnosed with PTSD, much like Nate had. But they didn't have any medical terms for such as that in the spiritual realm; you just dealt with it the best way you could, by asking the Creator for strength.

Faith's Legacy

Later that night Cleo had everyone who was still at the estate gathered into the den. Carl and Keelie had returned to Devon and Sabrina's house and Evan and Catherine had to return home for an appointment the next day. So, that left Charlie and Nate, Sabrina, Devon and the twins, and Savanna and Brody.

"I have a feeling deep in my spirit that bad things are happening in the spirit world. I'm not sure what it is, only that there is a shift. I gathered you all here tonight so that we could pray."

"Can you tell us exactly what we should be praying for?" Devon asked.

Cleo picked up her Bible and flipped the pages until she read from 2 Corinthians 10:3-5, "For though we live in the world, we do not wage war as the world does. The weapons we fight with are not weapons of the world. On the contrary, they have divine power to demolish strongholds. We demolish arguments and every pretension that sets itself up against the knowledge of God, and we take captive every thought to make it obedient to Christ."

Cleo closed her Bible and set it on the table next to the couch. "We are fighting a war. *There is a battle that goes unseen, between light and dark for you and me.* My grandmother used to quote that to me when I was just a child and again after I got involved with the occult. I have no idea if it was something that she came up with or if she was quoting someone else, but I always remembered it." Cleo sighed as she stared up at the ceiling, seemingly looking for guidance from above.

"The devil knows that we are the apple of God's eye. He knows that the only way to hurt God is to destroy us. That's why he goes after us so hard and he starts as soon as we are born. Why do you think that guardian angels are given to us? He gives us spiritual protectors to protect us from spiritual enemies. But we have a part to play in this battle as well. Our weapon is first and foremost this book right here." Cleo picked up her Bible and held it up high in the air.

"This right here is our best weapon, but if we don't know what's in here, it's like carrying around the sharpest sword in the world but never pulling it from its sheath. You must *use* it for it to work, but before you can use it you must first *know* it and then *believe* in it." She paused and then took a deep breath.

"We have been given authority over the devil. But what does that really mean? If you look up the word authority, it says this: *The power or right to give orders, make decisions, and enforce obedience.* The devil knows that as Christians and followers of Christ that we have been given this authority. He knows it, but he sure ain't gonna tell you if you don't know! He looks for weak Christians who don't know what power they have. He looks for those who would rather believe that he is simply a cartoon character running around in a red suit carrying a pitchfork, but he is very much alive and well, going about seeking whom he may devour." Cleo paused there for a moment. "Did you catch the key word there? I said he was seeking whom he *may* devour. That tells me that he can't just gobble up anyone he wants to. That tells me that there are some that he *may not* devour. I'm here to tell you right now that I am for sure one of those *may nots!*"

Luke got to his feet and stood before Cleo. "I want to be a *may not* as well, Cleo. Please teach me."

One by one every person in the room stood before Cleo and asked her to show them how to be a *may not!*

Charlie lay in bed staring up into the darkness. The soft rumble coming from Nate's side of the bed told her that he had found his escape from the worries of the day. She wished she could fall asleep so easily. Nate dropped off to sleep faster than anyone she had ever seen. Not that she had slept with too many people to be able to draw much of a comparison. But if her mom and her brothers and her friend Lakyn were anything to go by, Nate dozed off exceptionally fast. Sighing, she flipped back the covers and slid her feet to the floor. She absolutely hated not being able to sleep. She had read somewhere that if you don't fall asleep within thirty minutes of lying down that you should get up for least half an hour to reset your internal clock. She made her way down the hall and paused before starting down the stairs when a hard shove came from out of nowhere and sent her stumbling back against the wall just as a body flew past her head and tumbled down the stairs with a scream.

Gideon stared in shock at the body that lay lifeless at the bottom of the staircase. He just barely had time to knock Charlie out of the way when he saw Amaris come flying at her, intent on shoving her down the stairs.

"Oh, my Lord! Amaris!" Charlie cried out as she hurried down the stairs. Reaching out to turn her over, she stopped, remembering that she might do more harm than good by moving her. Charlie had no way of knowing if Amaris suffered any injuries to her back or neck. She lifted her right wrist and felt for a pulse. Panic took over when she couldn't detect one.

"Oh no...no... no... no! Nate! Mama! Devon! Someone heeelp!" she screamed out at the top of her lungs. Within seconds, Cleo's solid form came hurrying down the hall.

"Charlie! What on earth is the matter, child? You near scared me to death with your hollering."

"Oh, Cleo, it's so awful! I'm not sure how, but Amaris has fallen down the stairs! We need to call 911 right now!"

Cleo's eyes grew wide at the sight of Amaris's still body on the floor.

"Oh, sweet Jesus, help us." she said softly as she hurried to the kitchen to dial 911. Next Sabrina and Devon came out, followed by Brody and Savanna and finally Nate. Nate knelt next to Amaris and felt for a pulse then looked up at Devon, who shook his head, telling him he hadn't been able to feel one either. He really wished Hattie was still here, but she had gone back to California for a couple days to be with her family. At the moment, no one was at the estate but the family.

"Honey, what happened?" Nate asked.

Charlie wrapped her arms around her middle. "I'm really not sure. I was about to go down the stairs, but I stopped at the top for just a second to allow my eyes to fully adjust to the darkness when I felt someone push me away from the stairs and into the wall. The next thing I knew, Amaris literally came flying past me screaming as she fell down the stairs.

"So, Amaris didn't push you?" Nate questioned.

Faith's Legacy

Charlie shook her head, "No, she couldn't have. The push came from in front of me. I felt hands on each of my shoulders pushing back and to the side."

Every angel present looked at Gideon. "Amaris was going to push her down the stairs. When I saw what, she was about to do, all I could do was move Charlie out of the way. There was nothing I could do to save Amaris," he explained sadly.

"Why would she want to hurt Charlie?" Charlotte asked with a bewildered expression.

Gideon shook his head, "I have no idea, but you can bet that I will find out. I want every guardian sticking especially close to your human. We have no idea if this attack was the only one or only the beginning." He then turned to Mac. "I need you to go to her quarters. See what you can find that might give us a clue about why she would want to kill Charlie."

"Kill? Do you think that was really her intent?" Mac asked in dismay.

"Without a doubt. That's why she couldn't stop herself when I moved Charlie out of the way. She was running at full speed and had a look of cold rage on her face." Gideon glanced down at the floor where Amaris was still sprawled at an odd angle. He knew without touching her that her spirit had left her body.

The sound of sirens once more filled the night air at Lost Haven. The paramedics confirmed what they already suspected. Amaris had died, most likely from a broken neck. Since the fall resulted in a fatality, the police and the medical examiner were called.

"I'm going to go make some coffee; I don't think any of us will be going back to bed tonight," Cleo said as she sighed wearily then headed to the kitchen.

Charlie looked at Nate with tear-filled eyes. "What do I tell the police?"

"The truth, sweetheart. What else would you tell them?" Nate replied, wrapping his arms around her.

"What if they think I pushed her? I have no way of proving that I didn't."

Faith's Legacy

"They have no way of proving that you did, either," Nate pointed out. "Besides, I think she was going to push you, but you moved out of the way and she was unable to stop herself. I mean, think about it -- why would she come sailing past you like she did? Why was she moving so fast? She knew the stairs were there. She was intent on pushing you down the stairs, but when you moved unexpectedly, she couldn't stop herself and fell." Nate didn't think it was possible for Charlie's face to lose any more color but it did.

"You...you think she wanted to hurt me?" she stammered in shock.

"Honey, that's the only thing that makes any sense. If she were simply walking up behind you, she wouldn't have propelled herself down the stairs. She was coming at you fast to knock you down with as much force as she could. I think she was trying to kill you, not just hurt you." He pointed up the long flight of stairs. "A long fall from that is very likely to end in death, as you can see."

"But...that doesn't make any sense! Why on earth would she want to kill me? We have gotten along fine since we have moved in and I thought we were friends! She seemed so excited about all of our plans for this place." Charlie's voice broke on a sob as she fell into Nate's arms.

Sabrina stepped up and gently took Charlie from Nate. "Come with me, sweetheart. Let's go to the bathroom and wash your face. The police will be here soon." Charlie nodded as she hiccupped like she was three once more and allowed Sabrina to lead her to the bathroom.

"Honey, I'm going to go with them," Savanna said as she averted her eyes to keep from seeing the body again.

"Yeah, try to see if you can help Sabrina make Charlie understand everything will be all right," Brody said, giving her hand a soft squeeze.

Savanna sighed and shook her head. "Will it?" she asked then walked away before Brody could reply.

Devon studied the scene and then looked at Nate. "I keep coming up with the same scenario that you do. It's the only thing that makes sense, but we know Charlie and we know that she wouldn't hurt a fly. The cops, on the other hand, will be looking at her a little differently, I'm afraid, and with no witnesses it will be her word against the evidence."

"I think we should call Carl. Together with his law enforcement background and yours, maybe we can help the police see the truth," Nate said as he rubbed the back of his neck.

Devon nodded. "I will call the house and tell them what happened. I wish Evan and Catherine could have stayed tonight. I know that Charlie will need all the support she can get and she is very close with Catherine."

"So, call them. I know they will come back," Nate said.

"I know they would; that's why I'm not calling them." The look on his face made Nate pause his pacing.

"What are you not telling me?"

"They didn't want us to say anything until after the first of the year, but under the circumstances I feel it's best if you know. Catherine has been diagnosed with cervical cancer. She started her treatments last week. She didn't want to upset everyone right here at holiday time," Devon admitted with a grim look.

"I'm guessing she has another treatment tomorrow. That's why you didn't want to call. You knew she would come back here and miss it," Nate replied softly.

"Yeah, and I don't think we need to tell Charlie. Right now, she needs to concentrate on whatever all of this turns into."

"Do you really think this is going to become a big issue? I mean surely they will see it like we do."

Devon gave Brody a serious look. "When someone dies, it's always an issue." He raised his hand when Brody opened his mouth to explain what he meant.

"I know how you meant it, but I just meant what's obvious to us may not be to them," he explained.

Brody nodded, "I guess you're right. How about we pray before the house is overrun with people?"

"That sounds like a plan that I can get behind," Nate said as he reached for the hands of the other two men. Together they prayed for the soul of the woman who was on the floor, they prayed for Charlie's heart and mind, and they prayed for the police to see quickly the situation correctly and absolve Charlie from any responsibility.

"So, you say that no one else witnessed what happened? That it was only you and the deceased?" Officer Jenkins was writing notes on a small pad, looking up at Charlie often as she answered his questions.

"That's right, sir. I couldn't sleep so I was going downstairs to make some warm milk. I paused at the top of the stairs to let my eyes adjust to the darkness. Amaris came up behind me very fast and when I moved to the side, she fell down the stairs."

"Why did you move to the side? Did you hear her coming up behind you?"

Charlie looked at Nate with wide eyes. This was the part she worried about. How did she say that something or someone unseen had pushed her out of the way? She would sound crazy!

"Mrs. Jackson?" The officer looked at her with raised brows.

"I...I... don't exactly remember hearing her coming up behind, but I must have. It all happened so fast! I'm sorry I'm not clearer on exactly what happened," she finally answered.

"Hmm... do you have any reason to think that the deceased had any reason to push you down the steps?" he asked.

"Amaris," Charlie said with irritation.

"Pardon me?" the office looked up at her.

"Her name is Amaris; you keep calling her the deceased. She had a name, and to answer your question, no, I don't know of any reason for her to want to harm me or I, her. What happened here, officer, was a horrible, tragic accident." Charlie crossed her arms and fought hard to keep the tears at bay, but the investigator was making her see red and she knew that was never a good thing.

Officer Jenkins looked up at the stairs; then he went up the stairs and looked for a few minutes before coming back down.

"I think I have everything I need. It looks as if the medical examiner is about finished as well." He pulled out a business card and handed it to Charlie. "Be sure and call me if you can think of anything else." He turned to walk away then stopped and turned back to look at the group of people watching him. "Oh, and one more thing. I need all of you to stay in town for the next few days until this is all settled."

Gideon paced the roof of the estate with long strides and twitching wings. He was furious with himself for getting Charlie in this situation. It was his fault!

"Gideon, come on! You said yourself that you barely had time to get Charlie out of the way. What else could you do?" Zareck asked with a shake of his head.

"I don't know, but I should have reacted differently."

"You could have let Charlie be pushed down the stairs; that was about your only other option, as far as I can tell. Besides, we don't even know yet what the outcome will be. They have no probable cause for Charlie to try to kill Amaris."

"People don't just fall down stairs," Gideon said with a low growl.

"Uhh...yeah, G, they do, actually," Skye said.

Gideon fought hard to reign in his temper. "This looks suspect, very suspect. Charlie could very well be charged with murder." He turned to make another trek across the roof but came to an abrupt stop when Charlotte stepped directly into his path.

"Where's your faith, Gideon?" she asked softly. "Do you really think that our Creator will allow Charlie to go to prison? Can you stand there and look me in the eye and tell me that you *honestly* believe that will happen?"

Gideon's dark green eyes dueled with Charlotte's light green ones for a long minute before he finally bowed his head. "No. No, I can't," he admitted quietly.

Reaching up, Charlotte cupped his cheek with her palm, making him hold her firm gaze. "You did *your* job, warrior. You protected Charlie. Now let the Creator do *His* job and sort everything out."

Sighing deeply, Gideon offered the petite angel before him a small smile. "How is it that you always know how to reach through this thick skull of mine and make me see reason?"

Faith's Legacy

Zareck scoffed, "It's truly a gift, but I also think she knows she is the only one you won't knock flat for stepping up to you like that."

Mac shimmered into view just as Gideon nodded his head in agreement. "She would be correct."

Mac looked at Zareck with wide eyes. "What did I miss?"

Skye cracked up. "You missed Charlotte making Gideon heel like a good boy. It was great! All she needs to do now is give him a treat."

Charlotte frowned at the towering angel who was laughing. Snapping her fingers sharply, she pointed at him and gave him a stern look. Skye immediately hushed.

Spreading her wings wide, Charlotte gave a heavy down stroke to lift herself up into the air enough so she could pat the top of Skye's bare head.

"Good boy, Scooby!" The roof was filled with the sound of exploded laughter.

"So, what did you find out about Amaris?" Gideon asked.

"Well, it appears that our boy Karau has been very busy, and it didn't all have to do with Savanna either. Amaris was involved with some pretty dark stuff. Nothing like what Savanna was playing with but pretty messed up. She was placed here to keep an eye on Charlie and her family and most likely the estate as well."

"How did you find out all of this?" Zareck asked.

Mac held up a small spiral notebook. "From this."

Over the course of the next few days, Charlie was a nervous wreck. She kept watching for a police car to pull up and haul her off to jail. Unable to keep her mind on anything, she decided to go take a ride. It was now the first week of December, but she didn't care. Right now, frostbit fingers were preferable over a mind that was slowly going crazy. Pulling up, she saw her mom coming out of the house.

"Hi, what are you doing?" Charlie asked as she hurried up the steps.

"I was just coming to your house. I wanted to know if you had heard anything from the police yet."

Charlie shook her head, "No, that's why I was coming over here. I'm going nuts over there. I can't keep my mind on anything. I decided to take Stormy out for a while."

"You know, that sounds like a good idea. If I'm more worried about freezing to death, my mind won't be able to torment me with worrying about the outcome of all of this mess." Sabrina stepped off the porch and headed to the barn, leaving Charlie staring after her with her mouth hanging open.

"Hold up! You are going riding with me? On a *horse*?" she asked after she had caught up with her mother.

Sabrina laughed as she opened the stall door of her old mare Duchess. "Well, I'm certainly not walking while you ride. I think I can still remember how it's done." She turned and looked at Charlie sternly. "You just make sure you keep it at a decent pace, young lady. I'm certainly not up to your riding skill, so no racing!"

Charlie laughed as she led Stormy out of his stall.

"Yes, ma'am."

A few minutes later they left the protection of the barn and headed out across the pasture. Keeping her word, Charlie kept the pace nice and slow, although Stormy tossed his head and pulled hard at the bit. Finally, Charlie started loping him in wide circles around her mother and Duchess. Sabrina smiled but never asked Duchess for more than her sedate walk. Once Stormy had the restlessness run out of him, he was content to walk next to Duchess. Charlie and Sabrina chatted about everything except what was on both of their minds. Letting the horses pick the direction, the women didn't even notice where they were until Duchess stopped and snorted slightly. Sabrina looked around at the huge warehouse-type structure.

"What on earth is this?" she asked Charlie.

"I have no clue, Mama. I have never seen this before and I thought I had ridden everywhere on Devon's land."

Nudging Duchess closer, Sabrina looked at the tall round silos and what appeared to be a loading dock.

"Why, it looks like an old feed mill. I had no idea we had this on our property. I bet Devon doesn't either or he surely would have mentioned it."

Charlie nodded but didn't speak, for she was having her hands full controlling Stormy, who once more tossed his head and blew hard through his nostrils.

"Mom, I think we should go. Stormy must sense something bad about this place. See how he is blowing?" she pointed at her mother's horse. "Look, Duchess doesn't like it either."

Sure enough, while not acting out as much as Stormy, the old mare appeared to be watching something very intently and had gone very still with her ears pricked forward. Sabrina patted the mare's neck, "Okay, we can go. I don't think I like it either."

They both turned their mounts and headed back the way they had come, but what they didn't see was the swarm of black demons that exploded out of the old mill like bats…

Gideon shouted at Charlotte to stay with the women while he drew out his sword.

"No! You can't fight all of them alone!" she yelled back as she drew out her own sword. There was no more time for conversation, for the mass of minions had reached them.

Charlie struggled to control Stormy, who was now pawing the ground and fighting hard against the bit. He had never acted out like this before! It took everything she had to keep him in a fast trot. Looking back, she could see that Sabrina, too, was having a hard time keeping Duchess in hand. The old mare was high stepping and even tried to crow hop sideways.

"Mom! We have to go!" A feeling of extreme danger washed over her as she suddenly felt what the horses must have sensed the entire time. Sabrina looked up at Charlie and nodded her head to let Charlie know she understood.

"Drop the reins and hang on to the saddle horn! Duchess will follow us!" With that said, she eased off the pressure on the reins and Stormy took off like a bullet released from a gun. Charlie tried to keep the pace slow enough that Duchess could keep up, but it was a fight. Whatever was out there was scaring the crap out of her horse; it was doing a good job on her, too!

Sabrina held on to the saddle horn with all her might. Never had she ridden so fast. She never thought her old mare could produce this amount of speed. The wind whipped tears into her eyes so bad that all she could see of Charlie and Stormy was a blur in the distance.

"Oh, Jesus, help me hold on and keep us safe!" she prayed as she tried to see what was creating the overwhelming feeling of danger and fear, but she couldn't see anything.

Gideon tried to keep Charlotte, Charlie and Sabrina in his line of sight as they fought the host of demons that were coming at him from every side. Charlotte was doing remarkably well defending herself. Then Gideon noticed that Charlie and Sabrina were riding farther away and none of the black swarm was following. That's when he knew they weren't after their humans -- they were after them!

Raphael was sitting on the roof of the cabin when he saw the horses running for the house at a high rate of speed. If it had only been Charlie out riding, he wouldn't have thought much of it. That girl was always racing around on that high-spirited horse of hers, but it was the sight of Duchess, Sabrina's old mare, running like the hounds of hell were after her, that brought him to his feet.

"Zareck! Skye! We have trouble!" he shouted as he dove off the roof.

Faith's Legacy

Sabrina had never been so happy to see the cabin! Charlie pulled Stormy to a sliding stop just in front of the porch then jumped off to grab Duchess's bridle. The old mare's sides were heaving heavily from her unaccustomed exertions. But Charlie was too relieved to see her mother still in the saddle to worry over-much about the horse.

"Mama! Are you okay? Can you get down?" she asked.

Sabrina's face was white with fear, but she nodded her head and tried to let go of the saddle horn; however, her fingers were locked down over it in a white-knuckled grip. Devon came out of the house and took one look at his wife's face and knew something bad had happened.

"Honey, are you okay?" he asked as he placed his warm fingers over Sabrina's frozen ones.

Just the feel of his hand and the sound of his voice was enough to propel Sabrina out of the saddle and into his arms. Devon stumbled back a couple of steps but quickly adjusted his stance to support Sabrina's weight in his arms.

"Luke! DJ!" Devon called out. The twins appeared quickly. Boys, I need you to take care of the horses. They have been run hard. Especially look after Duchess; don't give her but just a little bit of water and rub her down real good."

The boys looked at the blown horses and the pale faces of the women who had ridden them and knew better than to ask too many questions.

Zareck and Raphael flew as fast as they could toward the old mill. They had left Skye behind to watch over the humans. They knew something terrible had happened because neither Gideon nor Charlotte returned with the women, and even as fast as the horses were running, there was no way they could run faster than the two guardians could fly.

Gideon finally pried his swollen eyes open enough to see that they were back in the old mill. His arms and legs were tied so tightly he had lost feeling in both his hands and feet. He turned his head, trying to see where Charlotte was. A sick feeling washed over him when he realized she was nowhere in sight.

    Charlotte knew two things when she woke up. One, she was hanging tied by her arms and she was hot...really hot. Was she in hell? Why was she so hot? Opening her eyes, she screamed in terror when she saw the red-hot pot of boiling metal under her dangling bare feet.

Chapter 23

Gideon felt his heart stop when the sound of bloodcurdling screams reached his ears. He wanted to scream himself. He wanted to tell them to let her go. They could melt him, if that's what they wanted to do, but not Charlotte, not sweet little Charlotte! He strained against his bindings again and again and yet again. He pulled with every ounce of strength he had, but his bonds held tight.

"Oh, mighty Creator! Why does this keep happening? Show me what to do!" He bowed his head in abject humility as he cried out, "I need you. I repent of my doubt. I repent of my disbelief. Forgive me, my Creator! Forgive me and help me be the warrior you made me to be! Let me defeat this enemy for **your** glory!"

Suddenly the bonds that had held him fast fell from his arms and legs. Gideon stumbled as he finally got to his feet. Looking around, he spotted his sword tossed carelessly over into a corner. Stooping down, he picked it up. As he rose to his full height, he felt the power of the Almighty wash over him, filling him with a strength that he had never known. Fire shot down through his muscles as it lent power to his limbs, sparks flew from his wings as his feathers sharpened all at once to razor- sharp points and his sword glowed with a white-hot flame that he knew was the Glory of God.

Karau walked around the pretty little angel that was dangling over the vat. Letting his gaze drift downward, he noticed her bare feet. For some reason that made him smile and just a bit curious.

"Now, I hope that you don't think that this is too forward; after all, we did just meet, but I do wonder why you don't wear any shoes."

Charlotte looked down at the demon smiling up at her in disbelief. He had her dangling over a pot of boiling iron and he wanted to know *why she wasn't wearing any shoes?*

"Well, why aren't you?" she asked with a roll of her eyes, then nodded to his clawed reptilian-like feet. "Because I'm telling you, if I had feet that ugly, I would definitely invest in some high-quality footwear."

Karau blinked in surprised. Why, the little angel was actually being sassy with him! Karau roared with laughter then looked up at the demon that was standing by with a pair of bolt cutters and nodded.

Gideon heard the snap and clink of the bolt cutters as they cut through the chains that held Charlotte suspended above the vat. A power unlike anything he had ever known poured into his body. His wings propelled him through the air with so much speed it was like watching everything in slow motion. He saw the chain snap as the cutters broke through them. He saw the expansion and retraction of the molecules as the iron was separated from the iron ore in the boiling vat. Charlotte's terrified scream filled the air with notes and vibrations of sound as she dropped toward the boiling iron. Feeling as if he had all the time in the world, Gideon turned his head to see where Karau was standing. He hoped he wouldn't be in too much trouble, but this demon was about to get a taste of his own medicine! Swooping down, he caught Charlotte with his right arm. With his left hand, he grabbed the red-hot rim of the vat and tipped it over, spilling its contents across the mill floor.

Karau stared in confusion at the streak of brilliant white light that flew across the room; then he screamed in horror at the tidal wave of crimson red that rolled over him...

Zareck and Raphael watched in uncomprehending disbelief as a blaze of white light that was Gideon tore through the remaining demons, his sword ablaze with a light unlike anything they had ever seen before. He was moving so fast that he looked more like a white whip flashing here and then over there. Scores of demon fiends fell like black rain into the boiling iron that covered the mill floor. He did all of this with one hand, for the other held a limp Charlotte firmly against his chest.

Finally, they were all gone. Every last demon in the mill, including Karau, was permanently and forever destroyed. Gideon stopped fighting. His chest felt tight and heavy as he tried to draw in enough oxygen. Suddenly feeling weak, he dropped to his knees, being careful not to harm Charlotte.

"Gideon? Are you all right?" Zareck asked as he knelt next to him, looking at him with concern. Unable to speak just yet, Gideon nodded. After a few minutes his heart rate slowed enough that he could tell them what happened.

Raphael looked at him with awe. "I have never seen anything like that in my entire existence!"

Zareck shook his head, "Nor have I. It was as if the power of our Creator was channeled through you. Truly it was beyond anything I have ever seen or heard of." The usual stone-faced warrior looked as star-struck as Raphael.

"Really? I'm glad you liked it, because I never want to do that again," Gideon said just before his eyes rolled to the back of his head and he went limp.

Weeks later Gideon had fully recovered and was feeling much like his old self. Everything was slowly starting to get straightened out in both the human world and his own. Charlie was cleared of any wrongdoing in the unfortunate death of Amaris, and even François was coaxed back into resuming his duty -- but only if he had a contract that stated in writing that he was the head chef, not Cleo. Gideon had a feeling that in the end the contract would be as worthless as the paper it was written on because he knew that Cleo would charm her way back into the kitchen.

Savanna and Brody had left to go back to California but would come back in the summer for their wedding, which they had decided to have at the estate. The medical wing was once more being worked on and Nate was excited to help Adam in his new business of making a better prosthesis. The only dark cloud was the fact that Catherine didn't seem to be responding well to her treatments, but it was still too early to know for sure what the outcome of that would be.

Thinking back to the day of Karau's ultimate demise, he knew he had learned a valuable lesson. Even he, an angel, could not defeat the enemy with doubt in his heart, for it was faith that produced the power and the strength to defeat any foe.

That is truly Faith's Legacy...

Keep reading for a preview of book 6 of *Saving Gideon: Chasing Hope.*

Chasing Hope

"Mom, are you sure you feel well enough to attend this wedding? I know Savanna and Brody will understand if you are too weak." Sabrina tried to reason with her mother, but Catherine was not having it. To look at her, you wouldn't think she would have enough strength to stand, much less argue with her daughter and give her hard looks.

"Sabrina, I can feel lousy just as easily while watching a beautiful wedding as I can lying in a bed. If given a choice, I would rather be distracted by a wedding, quite frankly."

Sabrina frowned. "Mother, I'm sorry. I didn't even think of it like that. If you want to go, I will do everything I can to make sure you are comfortable."

Catherine patted her hand. "It's all right, dear. Now why don't you send that handsome grandson of mine up here to help me down the stairs?"

Sabrina's lips twitched as she tried to fight off a grin. "Well, I'm afraid you're going to have to tell me which one you want, because you have two and being they are identical twins, they are both handsome."

Catherine smiled weakly as she reached up and adjusted the colorful head wrap that hid her bald scalp. "*Touché*, my dear, *touché*, you are correct. I do have two very fine grandsons whom I adore equally, but the one I was referring to was Luke."

"I will send him right up, "Sabrina said as she kissed her mother's cheek.

Minutes later there was a soft tap; then Luke stuck his head around the door.

"Hi, mama said you wanted me?"

Catherine smiled at Luke then patted the bed next to her. "Yes, dear, come in and sit down next to me."

Luke did as instruct, taking note of Catherine's pale face and thin body. He didn't know what was worse, the cancer or the treatments. "Are you feeling okay, Grandmother?"

Catherine smiled weakly. Luke was the only one of her grandchildren who called her Grandmother. Charlie and DJ both called her Mimi.

"I'm fine, sweetie. I just wanted to talk to you about something. Has your mother ever talked to you about your grandfather?"

Luke looked a little confused by her question. "About Grandpa Evan or Grandpa Carl?"

Catherine chuckled softly, "Well, perhaps I asked the wrong question. Let me try again. Has your mother ever spoken to you about her father?"

"Oh, no, ma'am, I don't believe so except to say that he died when she was young."

Catherine nodded. "Well, the reason I'm asking is there is something about you, a quality, perhaps, that reminds me very much of Sabrina's father."

"There is?" Luke asked with a small smile.

"Yes, you see people as they are, and you accept them in the same manner. Sabrina's father was like that. It was a trait that I'm ashamed to say I did not have until after your mother was grown." She stopped to catch her breath before continuing. "I guess I'm saying all of that to say this. I think you will make a wonderful missionary. I truly feel that the Lord has put within you the heart of a servant. I pray that the Lord will keep you and guide you in all of your adventures. But be aware that there are people out there who will have no problem taking advantage of a young man new to the ways of the world. The Bible tells us to be as harmless as doves but wise as serpents. In other words, don't trust everyone."

"You know that mama is dead set against me going to Cuba, don't you?" Luke asked with a sigh that said his heart was heavy over the matter.

"Yes, I know; more than that, I understand. A mother's heart is a difficult thing to have. Part of you is excited about your babies growing up and you're curious about who and what they will be, but then there is the part that wants them to stay children forever so you can watch over them and keep them safe. Be patient with her, Luke. She loves you so very much or this wouldn't be so difficult for her."

Luke nodded solemnly. "I know she does. That was never in question, and I love her, too. The last thing I would ever want to do is to hurt her, but I feel this calling to go to Cuba so strongly, Grandmother. I feel like I'm being torn apart!"

"Pray, my dear. Pray and ask the Lord for direction. He will never cause dissention in a family. If it's his will for you to go, he will make a way and he will calm your mother's heart."

"I have been praying. I pray every day, sometimes all day, about this, but Mama's heart is set against it. I can't even talk to her about it without her getting angry and upset."

Catherine cupped Luke's chin in her hand and stared into his eyes that were a perfect mixture of both Sabrina and Devon.

"That's when we pray the hardest prayer of all. Lord, your will be done."

The next morning Sabrina came downstairs to find Devon already up and dressed.

"Goodness, you must have gotten up with the chickens!" she said with a smile as she poured her cup of coffee.

"I was up early, that's for sure. Listen, why don't you sit down? I need to talk to you about something." The tone of Devon's voice had Sabrina setting the coffee cup down on the counter and facing him.

"What is it? Is it Mother? Has she…?" She stopped when she saw Devon shake his head.

"No, your mother is fine. That's not what I wanted to talk to you about. It's about Luke."

Feeling a wave of relief that her mother was okay, Sabrina picked up her coffee cup once more. Bringing it to her lips, she smiled.

Faith's Legacy

"What about him? Is he still trying to convince you to co-sign that car loan?"

Devon shook his head. The look on his face made Sabrina's stomach flutter uneasily. "No, it's not about the car."

"Well, for heaven's sake, what is it? You're starting to worry me."

"Honey, Luke is gone," Devon said flatly.

"Gone? What exactly do you mean by *gone*?" Sabrina asked carefully.

"I mean he is on his way to Cuba."

Sabrina felt the air leave her lungs in a rush before she remembered she hadn't signed the permission slip.

"Well, he may go to the airport, but they won't let him go. He is under age and I didn't sign the permission slip. So, he will be back," she said with a sigh. "I can't believe that he would try to sneak off like this. That's so unlike him."

"Sabrina, he didn't sneak off and he only needed one signature to be able to go," Devon said softly.

A sick feeling of dread washed over Sabrina as she stared at Devon. Placing the coffee cup carefully back on the counter, she licked her suddenly-dry lips.

"Devon, what are you saying?"

"That I signed the permission slip, I drove Luke to the airport and I watched him get on the plane to Cuba…"

Made in the USA
Columbia, SC
22 December 2021

51458523R00124